Lead Me Home

Lead Me Home

An African American's Guide Through the Grief Journey

CARLEEN BRICE

AVON BOOKS ◆ NEW YORK

AVON BOOKS, INC.
1350 Avenue of the Americas
New York, New York 10019

Copyright © 1999 by Carleen Brice
Cover illustration by Laurie LaFrance
Interior design by Kellan Peck
Published by arrangement with the author
ISBN: 0-380-79608-2
www.avonbooks.com

Library of Congress Cataloging in Publication Data:
Brice, Carleen, 1963–
   Lead me home : an African American's guide through the grief
journey / Carleen Brice.
      p.   cm.
Includes bibliographical references (p.).
1. Grief. 2. Loss (Psychology) 3. Afro-Americans. I. Title.
BF575.G7B7345   1999   99-33771
155.9'37'08996073—dc21   CIP

First Avon Books Trade Paperback Printing: November 1999

AVON TRADEMARK REG. U.S. PAT. OFF. AND IN OTHER COUNTRIES, MARCA REGISTRADA,
HECHO EN U.S.A.

Printed in the U.S.A.

OPM   10   9   8   7   6   5   4   3   2   1

For Grandmama and Papa

When you pass through the waters, I will be with you; and when you pass through the rivers, they will not sweep over you. When you walk through the fire, you will not be burned; the flames will not set you ablaze.

ISAIAH 43:2

Contents

Introduction 1

PART I · SORROW LIKE A SEA:
Absorbing the Shock of Loss 7

MEDITATIONS

EXERCISES

Acknowledgments

I wish I could say something more profound than "thank you" to all the people who helped me with this book. Please know that it means everything to me that you all wanted this book to happen as much as I did. Thank you to my agent Gareth Esersky, editors Lisa Considine, Chris Condry, Tia Maggini, copyeditor Chandra Sparks and cover illustrator Laurie LaFrance. Thanks to all the people who shared their stories of grief and recovery with me. Thanks to my fellow writers and friends who read the manuscript and offered helpful suggestions, encouragement and chocolate: Karen, Trina, Cara, Coleman, Steve, Wuanda, Susan, Debbie and Val. This book is more evidence that I make it through life by the grace of God and my friends. I send my love and gratitude to my family; much of this book is their story too, especially my brothers Charles and David. I want to offer my gratitude to Dirk for suffering through the writing of this book and being brave enough to marry me knowing that I hope to write others. Lastly, I give thanks that my mother's spirit lives on through her children and grandchildren, and give thanks to Sherry and Lovie for being my other mothers.

Lead Me Home

Introduction

On February 21, 1992, six days after her forty-fifth birthday, my mother died of breast cancer. I was twenty-eight years old and unprepared for the devastating crush of emotions that awaited me. I had always assumed my mother wouldn't die until we were both old. Old, wise and accepting of death.

My mother and I lived in different cities, and like many women, she kept the seriousness of her illness hidden. When she called me from the hospital—finally forced to admit the toll the disease had taken—I quit my job and took her home to die. I was with her as cancer made its final attack, spreading from breast to brain, consuming her body, stealing her sight. During the first week I was home, we chatted about television shows and celebrity gossip, anything that would distract us from the heavy tasks at hand.

But late at night, when the weight of what was happening would settle around us with the darkness, we confronted soul-searing matters like what might be waiting for her on the other side and what she still hoped to accomplish. In the hospital, she had talked with a wise pastor who reminded her that as long as she was breathing, she had a purpose. She told me she wanted to tell people "to live like they were going to die," meaning she wanted to share her profound awareness about the preciousness of each moment. She was hopeful she could eke out more time than her doctor forecasted, and we made plans for the months we thought she had left.

However, once cancer reaches your brain, it acts swiftly and mercilessly. She fell off quickly and was gone nineteen days after I arrived.

After she died, I hurt more than I ever thought possible. I sobbed so hard at times that I was unable to stand, or even sit up, often collapsing on the floor in a pool of tears. I was scatterbrained, forgetting where I was going while driving down the street. What mind I had left was full of fear. I expected everyone I loved to die at any moment. And when I wasn't afraid, I was angry. And when I wasn't angry, I felt guilty for not being a better daughter.

My reactions were part of a combination of feelings, thoughts and actions known as the grief process. I've since come to think of grief as a journey—a strange odyssey with a brutal beginning, an interminable, desperate middle and a spirit-restoring end. On this journey, we leave the safety of all that we have known and travel through terrifying, unfamiliar lands. It's in some ways similar to our ancestors' unwanted journey to America.

Our ancestors were able to survive and flourish against all odds and we can too. Even while facing unimaginable suffering as slaves, they found the strength to take up arms against their oppressors or to head north along the Underground Railroad. While being spat on, yelled at and physically attacked, black children found the strength to believe they had the right to the same education as white children and to walk into segregated schools. Medgar Evers, Martin Luther King, Jr., Malcolm X and countless others who we still mourn, found the strength to risk their lives for the struggle. Thank God we come from these people! People who made a way out of no way, which is what grief asks of us today.

It is with the strength we inherited from our ancestors that we will be able to make it to the other side of grief where we can build new lives. For our grief crossing ultimately leads us to another, higher place—a place where we have not simply moved on after our losses, but have also become wiser, healthier and stronger because of them.

After the shock and sadness of loss begin to fade, we have an unparalleled opportunity to experience deep spiritual, intellectual and emotional growth. When we are beaten up emotionally, we are more receptive to life's lessons. Alcoholics typically don't get sober until they hit bottom. Bodybuilders know the only way to build muscle up is to break it down first. That's what weight lifting is: strategically overworking a muscle so the fibers break down. Then, when the muscle is at rest, the body repairs itself and, in that process, the muscle becomes bigger and stronger.

A successful grief journey is important for everyone, but it is especially critical for African Americans. The pain of our individual wounds cuts deeper because of our collective losses. The legacy of slavery and racism has left scars on generations of souls. Despite the political, social and economic gains we've made in the last fifty years, we continue to face losses that come too often and hit too hard. We are targets of racially motivated violence. Drugs and violence devastate our communities. Illnesses like AIDS, cancer and heart disease strike us down at a disproportionately high rate.

Even those of us who haven't personally lost a loved one suffer. Every time a young black man falls to gun shots, every time a sister overdoses on drugs, every time one of us succumbs to any of the diseases that attack us with such vigor, our whole community loses that person's unique potential.

With so many losses, it's difficult to resolve our collective grief. Mental-health and medical experts (and what we know in our hearts) tell us that many of the illnesses and much of the violence African Americans suffer are direct results of the stresses we face. It's a horrible cycle: so many losses lead to unresolved grief, and unresolved grief causes more losses.

We must stop this cycle.

Marches, rallies, candlelight vigils and prayer meetings are examples of how people work together on a large scale to heal our communities. However, we also must pursue smaller, more personal expressions of grief, such as sharing our troubles with one another and making a personal commitment to working through our pain.

I offer *Lead Me Home: An African American's Guide Through the Grief Journey* to help you navigate the anguish, confusion, anger, loneliness, fear and remorse of bereavement. I have pointed out some twists and turns that I encountered along my way through grief and have also included insights from other people's grief journeys. I hope our experiences help you know that you are not alone. I also hope they help you recognize and learn the lessons of grief, for it has much to teach you about yourself and about life.

This book is divided into three sections, which reflect the beginning, middle and end of the grief journey. The first section, "Sorrow Like a Sea," describes the beginning of the journey, in which our task is to absorb the shock of loss. Section 2 is "The Middle Passage," which discusses how we come to adjust to life without our loved ones. The last section, "Welcoming Shores," details the end (as close as one gets to an ending) of the grief journey, with its renewed energy and optimism. Each section features meditations with inspirational and practical suggestions to help you "keep on keeping on" as you sojourn through grief, and exercises to help you put these ideas into action.

As you make your way through this book and your grief journey, remember that you *will* heal. With time, work and care I was able to learn from grief and reclaim myself from it. I made a home for myself fortified by my mother's gift of the awareness that life is finite. I crossed over into a new life that was without her, but brimming with passion, empathy and a much deeper appreciation of my blessings. Her death reminded me of the importance of living each day fully, with purpose and gratitude.

Grief may make it hard for you to focus, so take your time and be gentle with yourself. Just as the muscle needs time to repair, so do the spirit and the mind. Read this only a page at a time or if you really need to go slowly, read only the affirmations at the end of each meditation. Later you will be able to concentrate more, and then you can read through each section.

—⚈—

SORROW LIKE A SEA

Absorbing the Shock of Loss

We have come over a way that with tears

has been watered

We have come,

treading our path through the

blood of the slaughtered. . . .

"Lift Every Voice and Sing,"
JAMES WELDON JOHNSON

After the death of a loved one, we find ourselves in a place we do not know. Things are familiar, but deeply, irrevocably changed. Our families, friends, neighbors and coworkers seem to be speaking a language we no longer understand. The whole world is off-kilter; we have no balance. We feel dizzy, dazed, numb and nauseous. We are set adrift in a sea of sorrow, no longer anchored by our loved one's presence.

This is the beginning of the grief journey. At first, we stagger along in shock: Where are we? How can this be happening? Then slowly, painfully we move into denial, guilt, anger, fear, anxiety and a host of other emotions. We don't experience these feelings in a neat pattern; they roar in and out like waves.

Everyone's journey is different. For some, grieving might be a swift and melancholy trip through sweet memories. Others may travel rough waters for years. We do survive our losses, but we never, ever get over losing someone we love. Their loss is with us every day. The wound heals, but leaves a scar. A good friend of my mother's told me this and, because I knew instinctively that it was true, I trusted her advice and was able to hang on.

So trust me when I tell you that although you won't forget about your loss, and you won't "get over it," you *will* get through it. Hold that assurance in your heart as you embark on the first leg of your journey.

Meditations

SHOCK

Most often the first feeling we have when someone dies is shock, especially when the person dies unexpectedly. But even if the person was sick or old, his or her death may still come as a surprise. Death is so incomprehensibly final.

I felt like a zombie after my mother died. At her funeral, I thanked her friends and coworkers who came to pay their respects. I hugged people and shook hands, making sure family and friends were comfortable. I did not cry. I focused on others because I couldn't focus on myself. I couldn't yet accept the fact that my mother was gone. I was in shock.

We respond to emotional shock much like we do to a physical trauma. If we hurt our bodies, the muscles around the injury tighten protectively. When we're hurt emotionally, our minds and hearts freeze up to safeguard our spirits.

Do you feel numb, empty, frozen? Do you act like everything is fine, even though your life has just fallen apart? Do you feel like you're just going through the motions of life? If so, you're probably in shock.

And that's OK. Shock is helpful. It's a way of protecting yourself, allowing yourself time to absorb what's happened. This aspect of grief will last only as long as you need it to. Your mind and heart are wise: You will start to feel when you are ready. Don't be afraid of the thaw. When it happens, you'll be strong enough to handle it.

I allow myself time to absorb what has happened.

DENIAL

Denial is very much like shock. At one level we know our loved ones are gone, but on another level we aren't yet ready to accept that reality.

My mother died while I was at the funeral parlor picking out her casket. When I returned, my brother met me at the front door and hugged me. "She's gone," he said. "Mama's gone." My first thought was, "Gone where? She's too sick to go anywhere." It took a minute for me to realize that he meant she was dead. Mama's dead.

I went upstairs and sat next to her. She wasn't breathing and her eyes weren't completely closed. Clearly, she was dead, but I still didn't believe it.

Not even after the funeral and seeing her body in the coffin. Not even after dividing her belongings among friends and family. For weeks, I expected her to call me and tell me that it had been some horrible mistake, a cruel joke. For months, I woke up hoping it all had been a bad dream.

If you can't believe this is happening—if it doesn't seem real—don't worry. You're not losing your mind. Just because you find yourself unable to believe your loved one is dead doesn't mean you are crazy. It just means you are crazed with grief. It's completely normal to expect your loved one to walk in from work in the evening or to come to the breakfast table in the morning.

You may be used to missing people for short times: when you moved to a new city, when a loved one went away to college, after you broke up with your high school sweetheart. But missing someone *forever*? There is no way to be prepared for a loss of that magnitude.

You are facing one of life's most difficult and profound challenges. Give yourself time to adjust. Take it slow. Go easy on yourself. Soon enough the reality of what has happened will settle in.

I am strong enough to accept the truth.

DISORDER
—∾⁓—

As the ice around your heart melts, fear, resentment, doubt, relief, anger and sadness may wash over you in such a massive wave that it feels impossible to separate one feeling from another. Before, you weren't able to comprehend your loss, now it's all you can think about.

But there is so much that requires your attention. The rest of the world is moving along normally, and even though your world has ended, you must keep going. You may still have children to care for, a job, a house or school. Keeping up with these demands may make you feel confused and lost. A simple trip to the grocery store can become a great chore. Choices that you used to make effortlessly now feel monumental. What to make for dinner? What to wear to work? Impossible decisions.

Soon after a loss, people misplace things, overlook appointments, forget what day it is. I locked myself out of my car three times in the first few months after my mother died. At my grief support group, the counselors ended each session by reminding us to think a few minutes about where we were going before we went to our cars, but I still often lost my way when driving home.

Our minds wander so easily when we are grieving.

Remind yourself to stay focused on the task at hand. Be careful not to hurt yourself. While you're driving, try to pay attention to traffic. When you're working in the kitchen, be careful of the stove, hot water and sharp objects.

Most grievers are very spacey. If you're forgetful, carry a small notebook. Write down grocery lists, appointments, when bills are due, etc. Make a spare set of keys. Ask people to call and remind you if you are supposed to meet them. Ask family members or roommates to help keep track of household activities like shopping, cleaning and mowing the lawn.

This part of the grief journey is frustrating, but be patient. Your inner world is a jumble, and your outer world only reflects the chaos within. Do what you can to keep order and take care of business, but don't worry about the messiness. Cut yourself a lot of slack; beating up on yourself won't help. You'll get your bearings again.

Disorder is only a temporary state. I know calm will come again.

Feeling angry may also be part of your grief journey. It's natural to protest against death, as we almost always think it comes too soon. It's common to be mad at medical professionals who couldn't save our loved ones. It's even normal to be angry with God and to question our faith. How could God allow plane crashes, bombings, gang fights, diseases and destruction? Why would God take our mothers, our sons, our lovers?

For African Americans, anger is especially warranted. How can we not be infuriated when diseases claim higher percentages of blacks than whites? How can we not be outraged by the senseless violence that claims too many young lives? How can we not be enraged by the continued racist attacks and murders of African Americans simply because of our skin color? Too often, deaths in our communities could have been prevented. Better nutrition, more access to health care, safer streets and economic opportunities could eliminate so much heartache. And avoidable misfortune is a bitter pill to swallow.

But anger takes a toll. If we don't acknowledge and deal with our fury, we will turn it on ourselves or vent it on others. Holding on to it can also make us sick. We must find healthy ways to express anger: Hit a pillow, write in a journal, talk it out, get in a car and scream or go for a brisk walk.

If you feel helpless and frustrated, use your anger to help you. Write letters to elected officials. Volunteer to work for organizations like Parents of Murdered Children, Mothers Against Drunk Drivers or Mad Dads. Righteous indignation can change things.

It is healthy for me to express all of my emotions, including anger.

GUILT

We may be angry with ourselves after the death of a loved one. Angry that we didn't protect them from illness, injury, death. Self-directed anger carries enormous feelings of guilt and regret. It's hard to accept that there will be no second chances, no more opportunities to help our loved ones, to be kinder to them, to tell them how we feel. We dwell on all the ways we could have done better. Sometimes we feel guilty simply for surviving our loved ones. Why did they die and not us? What right do we have to be alive, let alone be happy?

Even the little things we wished we would have done haunt us. In her autobiography, *Don't Block the Blessings*, Patti LaBelle talks about how guilty she felt for not making one of her sisters an egg sandwich before she died. Like Ms. LaBelle, I couldn't stop remembering a request of my mother's. She wanted me to visit for Thanksgiving, but I was going for Christmas and didn't want to make the long drive twice in one month. I was stressed out and broke and wanted to spend Thanksgiving with my then-boyfriend's family. Plus, I didn't know how very sick she was. Still, she asked me to come and I said no.

But that's only the beginning of what I felt guilty about. The day my mother died I woke up to hear her wailing in distress. I called the hospice nurse to try to get more medication for her, but it was too late. My sister-in-law said she died with a lot of thrashing and moaning—not the quiet good night I wanted for her. I felt enormously guilty for not being there when she needed me. I felt like I should have known ahead of time to give her more drugs; I should have heard her cries sooner. (I've since learned that death is not like it is in the movies. Many people who die from an illness like cancer do not go peacefully.)

It may be a while before you stop feeling guilty. No matter how illogical it seems, guilt is part of the process. It took more than a year before I stopped blaming myself for how my mother died. Eventually, I was able to accept that I couldn't change the past, and I was able to believe that I did the best I could. We all could have been better children, siblings, partners, parents, friends. No matter what you did for your loved one, you could have done more, but try not to let the "could haves" and "should haves" eat you up. You did the best you could. Your loved one knows that.

Try to forgive yourself by remembering what the Qur'an says, ". . . Allah will love you and forgive you your faults, and Allah is Forgiving, Merciful." Also, remember your kindnesses. Try to focus on what you did for your loved one. If your loved one died while you were at odds, remember the time before that when things were good between you. All relationships have ups and downs.

We can't change history, but we can learn from it. We can make sure we don't repeat the same mistakes.

Is there someone you want to make peace with? Is there something you need to tell a relative or a friend? Use your guilty feelings in a positive way and focus on what you can still change.

I forgive myself as God and my loved one forgive me.

BARGAINING
—⁄⁄⁄—

You know what bargaining is. It's when you promise that if you get through a certain problem, you'll try to be a better person. Maybe you swear never to curse, cheat or lie again. ("Please God, don't let me get a ticket and I'll never speed again." "If this check doesn't bounce, I'll balance my checkbook every month.")

Grieving people might say something like "Please God, bring my loved one back and take me instead." Or "Please God, I'll dedicate my life to you if you just give me one more chance with my loved one." It doesn't make much sense to our logical minds, but our pain is so deep that we'll grasp at any hope to have our loved ones again. Indeed, denial and shock are a part of bargaining. It's common to pray that your loved one didn't die. To yearn for him so much that you beg him to return. While it is irrational, trying to bargain to bring back our loved ones is often a part of the healing process. Eventually, you will accept that no matter what you do, your loved one isn't coming back. In the meantime, be easy on yourself. Accept all your reactions as natural and normal.

I may not always understand my thoughts and feelings, but I accept them as a necessary part of my healing.

FEAR

This is a frightening journey. Our awareness of death is so heightened that all the dangers of the world seem imminent. We may become consumed with all the ways it is possible to die. We may be afraid we'll get the disease that killed our loved ones. We may be afraid to ride in planes or cars if our loved ones were killed in an accident. Or we may simply feel suspicious of goodness and happiness. After all, we have evidence that joy can be snatched away at any moment. After my mother died, fear colored my view of life. I just knew all my other loved ones were going to die soon too. I actually fretted over the health of my plants.

Too often, black folks refuse to admit we are afraid. We have learned that being afraid means being vulnerable, and that conceding weakness puts us at risk. However, by denying our fears, we risk causing ourselves even more pain. We forget that fear loses power when it is acknowledged and expressed.

It's OK to be afraid, especially in the face of your loss. Don't be embarrassed by or ashamed of your anxieties. Choose safe ways of dealing with your fears. Treat yourself as you would a child who is afraid of the dark, and do things that make you feel safe. Ask your ancestors, spirit guides, Allah, Jesus, Buddha, Isis, Oludumare or the person who passed away to protect and guide you. If you still feel overwhelmed by fears, it might help to talk to other mourners, grief counselors or religious advisers.

I am strong enough to admit when I'm afraid and find loving ways to take care of myself.

COMPLICATED GRIEF

Sometimes grief includes issues that make the journey more complicated than usual. For example, finding the body, seeing the person die or being in the same accident or disaster as the person who died adds another dimension of trauma. High-profile murders or accidents, or other unusual deaths often attract attention that can make grief harder to bear.

If you are grieving such a loss, it's even more important to make sure you have support. Consider seeing a grief counselor or therapist or joining a grief support group. Talking with a therapist or with people in your situation can be cathartic and enormously helpful in accepting and sorting through complexities. The following meditations offer specific information on situations that make grieving harder.

GRIEVING SOMEONE WHO HURT YOU

Sometimes we are in the position of grieving someone who hurt us—a parent who abused us, a spouse who cheated on us or a friend who betrayed us. When we have been hurt by someone who dies, we may feel a baffling combination of hatred, love, anger and sadness at their loss.

It's difficult enough to reconcile such mixed emotions, but to make matters worse, other survivors may not share our perceptions. They may not have had bad experiences with the person or may be unwilling to face their negative feelings. And even if they do empathize with us, they may feel uncomfortable speaking ill of the dead.

Though you may share a sense of loss with other mourners, it may be hard to listen to them sing the praises of the deceased. Because you cannot pretend the deceased was perfect, you may feel at odds with your loved ones. The other survivors may not approve of or accept how you feel, making you feel sadder and more lonely. Ignore what they think because if the deceased hurt you, you will have unfinished business and it can make your grief process more confusing and painful.

To sort through your emotions write them in a journal or talk about them with a friend. Most important, allow yourself to feel all your emotions. You have the right to honor your experience with the deceased. You don't have to pretend to feel good about him. If you don't want to participate in mourning rituals with your relatives, you don't have to. However, don't let your own anger or hurt feelings make you hurt someone else. Simply explain to other mourners that your feelings about the deceased are different, and you'd rather not join them.

If you choose not to mourn with others, you'll still need to mourn in a way that feels right to you. After all, even though the person hurt you, you have experienced a loss. You will need to mourn the fact that the person won't have the chance to apologize or make amends. You will need to mourn any hope of having the relationship with him that you wanted and deserved.

The loss of someone who hurt you can be quite painful if you cannot console yourself with warm memories or share your feelings with your loved ones. However, you can get through all the conflicting emotions and get on with your life. And enjoying your life is the best way to right the wrong that was done to you.

I am true to my experience with the person who passed away.

GRIEVING A VIOLENT DEATH

While any death is somewhat of a shock to the senses, death by violence is a complete outrage. The murder of someone you love makes you doubt everything you've known to be good and true. It can rob you of your faith and trust in people and in God. Sadly, too many of us find ourselves trying to comprehend the incomprehensible: More than half of the people killed in this country every year are African American (although we make up only about 12 percent of the population).

Homicide bereavement often lasts longer and is more complicated than grieving natural deaths. Losing someone to murder brings on horror, shock, fear and helplessness in measures too large for even the strongest person. In addition to the magnified emotions of grief, those who mourn a murdered loved one often feel surrounded by strangers—police officers, lawyers, social service agencies and reporters—and abandoned by their friends. The stigma of murder may make people avoid you.

Security is also a big issue for survivors. It may seem impossible to feel safe after a loved one was killed by a drunk driver, in a robbery or after being sexually assaulted.

The anger many grieving people feel can become

rage. Survivors want justice, and they might also want revenge: "an eye for an eye."

The emotions after someone you love is murdered are so intense that it's almost impossible to bear them on your own. Don't try to go it alone. Be kind enough to yourself to get support from someone who understands the unique nature of your grief. Check with the police department, district attorney's office or social service agencies to find a victims' assistance program, support group or counselor.

It also helps people get through homicide bereavement to try to bring justice for their loved ones, educate lawmakers or help others who have lost someone to murder. For example, after her daughter was raped and murdered, Dee Sumpter founded Mothers of Murdered Offspring (MOM-O). MOM-O is part support group for people who have lost family members to homicide and part community organization taking action to prevent violence.

Ms. Sumpter says the years since her daughter's death feel like minutes. She believes she won't have complete closure until she joins her daughter in Heaven, but she also states her spiritual walk has grown more meaningful and she "has learned to thank God even in the darkest moments."

By sharing their feelings and reaching out to others homicide survivors *can* heal and lead complete, happy lives again. As Wanda Henry-Jenkins said in her book *Just Us: Overcoming and Understanding Homicidal Loss and Grief*, "The murderers may have diminished our joy but they will never steal our souls and kill our minds."

I know I can heal from this loss and trust in life again.

GRIEVING A DEATH FROM AIDS

As our society becomes increasingly familiar with AIDS, the stereotypes surrounding it are slowly disappearing. However, people still tend to blame the victim for contracting the disease. We continue to perceive people who get the virus from blood transfusions or from their mothers as "innocent" casualties, while viewing those who get the disease in other ways as having brought it on themselves. These misperceptions can cause mourners to feel like they must justify their grief. It's a form of discrimination that most bereaved people don't have to face.

In addition to negative reactions from others, mourners may be uncomfortable with their loved one's sexual orientation or drug use. They may be embarrassed to talk about the loss of their loved ones, and talking about grief is crucial to recovering from it.

Life partners face additional pressures. They may worry about their own health. They may feel intensely guilty for having passed the virus to their lost lover. Gay men may be excluded from grief rituals by their lovers' families. In her book *Recovering from the Loss of a Loved One to AIDS*, Katherine Fair Donnelly points out that frequently "Lovers and life partners are viewed as a friend or a roommate . . ." instead of spouses, which disregards the deep pain they feel.

Don't be ashamed of your loved one or your loss. No matter how the person got the virus, you still have the right to grieve. Don't let anybody take that away from you.

Because of the myriad sensitive issues in grieving an AIDS death, lovers, families and friends really should seek support from other people who have lost someone to AIDS. It will help to know you are not alone. Contact your local hospice or AIDS organizations for support groups.

It also can be helpful for people who have lost someone to AIDS to get involved in the many organizations pushing for research funding or supporting those who suffer from the disease.

And though it doesn't help your loved one, maybe it can be some comfort that new treatments for AIDS are being developed to help others. I know I feel better when I hear about research and treatments for breast cancer that may save someone's life.

I grieve my loved one with love and pride, and I know I will survive this loss.

There is an old wives' tale that black folks don't commit suicide. But as many of us so painfully know, we can no longer fool ourselves with that misconception. No race is immune to the despair and desperation that drives someone to take his own life. Indeed, the Centers for Disease Control and Prevention has reported that suicide rates are on the rise for African Americans, particularly our young men.

Deaths by suicide carry a stigma that make the grief journey rockier. Mourners may not know why their loved ones killed themselves, leaving them searching for answers. Even if the person left behind a note, it can still be frustrating and unbearably impossible to understand. The survivors often feel responsible and guilty that they didn't prevent their loved ones from taking their lives.

Don't punish yourself for your loved one's suicide; you did not cause it. Most people kill themselves because they are clinically depressed and believe ending their lives is the only way to end their agony. If the person threatened suicide as emotional blackmail, and you didn't believe him, you still shouldn't blame yourself. You cannot hold yourself responsible for the choices another person makes. Be honest about how your loved one died. When people ask, you can keep it simple, but tell the truth. You have nothing to feel ashamed or guilty about.

Help yourself by learning more about depression and mental illness. Read books, speak to a therapist or join a suicide survivors' support group. As with mourning other deaths, it is also helpful to write a letter to the person who passed away. In your letter, ask why she did it, ask for forgiveness, offer your forgiveness and wish her peace.

Another way to soothe your guilt and find some meaning in your tragedy is to try to help others who mourn someone who committed suicide or to help people who might be considering suicide. For example, Les Franklin, whose teenage son Shaka killed himself, quit his high-powered corporate job to spend more time with his family and start the Shaka Franklin Foundation for Youth. The nonprofit organization sponsors youth and family programs in an effort to prevent child and teen suicides.

Be gentle with yourself as you mourn your loss. Understand that you may feel a host of strange and confusing feelings—everything from anger to remorse to sorrow to shame. Whatever you feel is a normal reaction to such a devastating blow. However, if you contemplate taking your own life, talk to a mental-health counselor right away. You know how this suicide has affected you. Don't make someone you love feel the same way.

You'll never get past it, but you *can* work through your grief.

I am strong enough to mourn and survive my loved one's suicide.

GRIEVING MULTIPLE DEATHS

Sometimes lightning does strike the same place twice or even three or four times. Car accidents, plane crashes, tornadoes, fires and other disasters can claim the lives of several loved ones at once, wiping out a family. Or within a short period, we can lose one loved one after another.

Grieving multiple losses can be overwhelming and may make your grief journey more difficult. Each loss is its own tragedy, but when added together, multiple losses become even more difficult to handle. There is a danger that we will lose the ability to see each loss for what it is and only see one giant wound that feels impossible to heal.

The key to recovering from accumulated losses is to mourn each one individually. Just as each person was unique, and our relationship to each was different, each loss will mean something different. You might want to divide your grieving time into blocks dedicated to each person you lost. For example, you can specify a half hour of time in the morning to feel and think specifically about your father and then spend a half hour later in the day to concentrate on your sister. Light a candle for each person. Plant a tree, rosebush or sunflower in honor of each person.

Another good way to give each loss meaning is to start a memory collection for each of the people you've lost. You can use a scrapbook, photo album or even a shoe box. Include photos, letters, news clippings and other keepsakes. Try to make each collection specific to the personality of your loved one. Separating memorabilia will help you separate your feelings connected to each person's loss.

Also give yourself plenty of time to grieve each of your losses. Be patient and gentle.

By thoroughly grieving each of my losses, I know I can survive them.

GRIEVING A CHILD

Bereaved people often ask "why?" but the death of a child seems to beg the question even more. Parents have such impossible expectations to live up to: They are supposed to protect their children from all harm and love them through all despair. Above all, they're not supposed to outlive their children. It's the natural progression of life. Children are not supposed to die before their parents.

But tragically, for reasons none of us can know, life sometimes works outside the natural order and a child dies before her parents. Even when your child is grown, it still goes against reason for a parent to outlive a child. After the death of a child, the shock and denial phases of grief will be prolonged. It takes a long time for the mind to reconcile the awful reality of such a loss.

When a child dies, parents lose so much. You lose your identity as a mother or father. You lose the future you envisioned for yourself, and the future you wished for your child before you even knew her—going to school, getting a job, marrying and having children. In addition, we think of our children as our legacy, so when we lose them, we lose our futures. In the most literal sense, we lose a part of ourselves.

Parents, grandparents and siblings often feel incredibly guilty after the death of a child. Parents and grandparents may feel like they should have been able to protect the child from illness or accidents. Siblings often feel guilty for surviving a brother or sister.

It will help to acknowledge and accept your feelings of guilt. No parent is perfect, and almost all grieving parents feel like they failed their child. Unresolved guilt and blame can destroy individuals, marriages and families. A child's death often causes or exacerbates problems in a marriage. That's why it is so important to talk about how you're feeling. Men and women grieve differently and fathers and mothers have different relationships with their children. Though you both feel sorrow, guilt and anger, it could show itself in different ways that each of you could misinterpret. You could mistake your spouse's silence for rejection or think he's angry at you when he's angry about the loss.

In addition, you will need to pay attention to your relationships with your surviving children. Help younger children remember that you love them and don't blame them for your sadness. Be aware that children may feel guilty, confused or unable to cope. Try to help your children understand that they did not cause your sorrow, nor are they responsible for "fixing" things in the family.

Include friends and family in mourning rituals. Grandparents, siblings, aunts, uncles, cousins, godparents, baby-sitters, schoolmates and neighbors need to express their grief too.

After the death of a child, things will never be the same again. It could take years to complete your grief journey. But you *can* go on.

My child lives on in my heart forever.

GRIEVING A PARENT OR GRANDPARENT

Very often, when we lose an elder, we are discouraged from grieving "too much." After all, they are supposed to die before us. It is life's pattern: One generation falls back to clear a path for the next. However, that doesn't mean it doesn't hurt.

And it doesn't mean we will be ready for it. We may do some anticipatory grieving as our parents and grandparents age and decline. But even with the reminders that death is coming, it can still be hard for us. We'll still miss the daddy who used to play with us or the mama who could kiss life's hurts away or the grandfather who had all the answers. We may surprise ourselves with the depths of our emotions, particularly if the parent was elderly. Though it's comforting to know the person lived a full, long life, we may still want them with us. No matter how old we are, as long as our parents are alive, we are still their children. When they die, we feel orphaned. My friend Mattie says her mother's loss is "a hurt I can't explain. Nobody ever takes the place of your mother." Indeed, the parent-child relationship is unique; we only get one mother and one father.

The death of a grandparent could mean the loss of the head of the family, the glue that held the family together and the keeper of the family history. Also, many African Americans are raised—at least in part—by our grandparents, which makes our relationship with them even closer.

Wearing jewelry or clothing that belonged to your parent or grandparent can be soothing and a tribute to how much they meant to you. My friend Wuanda wears her father's shirts to feel close to him. I have some of my mother's jewelry that I wear when I want to keep her spirit close.

As with other losses, it's helpful to talk to people about your grief. You'll find that others who have lost a parent will understand how you feel. Don't be embarrassed or ashamed of feeling childish. After my mother died, I wanted my mommy. I wanted the comforting and assurance that only a parent can provide. Mourning a parent is as valid as mourning any other loss. No matter how old your mother or father was—no matter how old you are—you still have the right to grieve and mourn. Even people in their sixties will grieve the loss of their eighty-year-old parents. There's no age limit on grief.

Accept how you feel and give yourself permission to grieve. And remember that your parent lives on in you.

I am the strength, love and hope of my elders; their spirits will guide me the rest of my days.

When two people get together, they (consciously and subconsciously) take on different roles. Often, women assume responsibility for the emotional well-being and health of the family. They are the nurturers and communicators, in charge of the social structure of the family—keeping track of basketball games, soccer practices, church picnics and doctors' appointments. Men often provide safety and security for their families, and, even in our community where so many women work, often carry heavy financial burdens. Both roles are needed to keep the family going. When one of the partners dies, the other not only has to deal with the pain of the loss, the remaining partner also has to take on the overwhelming task of the other's duties. Suddenly, only one oar is in the water but the boat still must be rowed.

In addition to the stress of maintaining dual roles, you may have to adjust to living alone and sleeping alone for the first time in years. You may have to learn to make parenting and financial decisions on your own. You may have to adjust to celibacy until your grief is healed, then face an unfamiliar world of dating.

The loneliness of grief is even more profound when you lose a mate. Another hardship that widows, in particular, face is feeling socially neglected. My friend Velma said that her biggest disappointment after her husband died was that her friends no longer invited her to dinner or parties because they were afraid to have a single woman around their men.

If you've lost a lover, your grief may be discounted by others. The death of a boyfriend or girlfriend sometimes isn't considered as important as the death of a husband or wife. However, the loss of a beloved partner is always distressing. You have the right to grieve this devastating loss.

It may seem insignificant, but changing little things like moving the furniture in the bedroom or getting a new bed or sleeping on the couch or in the guest room can help for a while.

Another thing that may help, that many widows and widowers sorely miss, is touch. Our skin is our largest organ, and we definitely benefit from regular human contact. Give friends and relatives hugs, and ask them to hug you. Treat yourself to massages as often as you can afford.

Remember to honor your emotions and take care of yourself.

Even without my "other half," I am whole and complete, and I will survive this loss.

TELL YOUR GRIEF STORY
—⚡—

Talking about the death of a loved one is a natural, healthy part of grief. As a matter of fact, talking about it again and again is crucial to surviving a loss. No matter what the trauma, people benefit from going over what happened many times. In 12-step groups, they call it "telling your story."

In the months after my mother died, I talked about her illness and death incessantly. After a while, those around me stopped wanting to hear about it. They simply weren't as obsessed with every detail of every minute of her last days as I was. Also, death makes people uncomfortable. It upset people who didn't want to imagine what it would be like to lose their own mothers. It disturbed those who had ungrieved losses in their past.

Saying how we feel might make us anxious. It might make other people feel uneasy. But we need to express the shock and awe that we feel about the depth of our pain. We need someone to bear witness to it. Being honest about how we feel frees us. Let's be clear: Grief just plain stinks! Greeting-card sentiments and movie dialogue can't begin to describe the enormity of loss. Acknowledging the awful reality of what it is like to lose someone lightens the load we carry.

To find more receptive listeners to my grief story, I joined a support group. I felt understood when I shared silly, shameful or disturbing emotions with people who were traveling the same journey.

Find someone you can talk to. Every person will experience bereavement somewhat differently, but you can bet that somebody, somewhere has been where you are today. Let that be some comfort: You're not alone. Even if they don't feel the same as you, people in your shoes will at least be more likely to understand.

Shout your story from the highest mountains and whisper it in grief's darkest caves.

I speak up about how I feel.

GRIEVE AT YOUR OWN PACE

One of the keys to any successful journey is pacing yourself. I wish I could tell you that a certain number of days or definite amount of crying, thinking or praying about your loss would end your heartache, but I can't. There is no specific formula for healing; it takes what it takes.

I used to keep track of how long it had been since my mother died, hoping that I would reach some magic point (Three months? Six months? A year?) when it wouldn't hurt so much. I didn't experience healing in one flash, but with time and work, I did feel better. I can promise you that you will too. But I can't tell you when.

Do what is right for you. If you are ready to sing in the sunshine today, do it, no matter how recently your loved one died. If you feel sad and depressed and people are telling you to cheer up, ignore them. You have the right to grieve at whatever speed comes naturally.

I set my own pace through grief.

People grieve differently. Some scream and cry and moan. Some suffer silently. Some may not suffer at all. It depends on your relationship with the person who died. It depends on your personality. It depends on your gender. It depends on the circumstances of the death.

Where will your grief journey take you? Nobody knows. While there are some common traits among those who grieve, there is no perfect road to follow. There is no right way to grieve.

I heard a Buddhist master say that if we truly accepted the impermanence of life, we would see death as a natural occurrence. And, because death is a part of life, death shouldn't be experienced as loss. African-American culture also holds that death is natural, even something that should be welcomed, as it means we're leaving the tribulation of this world behind and going to a better place.

What, then, does this say about the grief journey? I'm sure that those who are more spiritually evolved can accept death without the shock and sorrow I felt. There are even people who are able to celebrate when their loved ones cross over.

But I also know we can't let go of something until we are ready. It wouldn't do any good to pretend to find joy in somebody "going home" if you don't feel happy. It won't help to tell yourself "He wouldn't want me to be sad" if you feel like crying your guts out.

Do what you need to do. The Buddhist teacher told his audience to let go. Without a doubt, I held on. I held on for dear life when my mother was dying, and continued to cling to her long after she was dead. I held on to her even after she came to me in a dream and told me she was happy and free.

Do what you need to do to get through this. Look to others for solace or inspiration, but you know how you need to grieve. Loud and wild or slow and quiet. Find your own way. When it comes to your grief walk, *you* are the expert.

I know what I need to do to heal.

TRUST YOUR FEELINGS

We are ultrasensitive after a loss. It can feel like we're walking around with no skin on; the slightest offense wounds us deeply. Things we used to shrug off may make us cry or argue now. We should be careful about jumping to conclusions around our family and friends. We can even almost safely assume that—especially in the first few months after a loss—we are probably overreacting. Chances are the people around you don't even know they are upsetting you.

But just because we should think twice before we react doesn't mean we shouldn't trust how we feel about our loss. We need never doubt our feelings for our loved one or our feelings about their death. Honor your emotions and trust your inner voice.

Many of us have been taught not to "put our business on the street," and, therefore, don't know how to deal with our feelings—especially "bad" feelings like fear, shame, anger, envy and sadness—so we avoid them. Dealing with emotions can be frightening at any time, but after a loss, when we are faced with so many feelings at once, it's overwhelming. It feels easier to ignore our pain.

But it's not. The only way to handle our emotions is to express them. We don't have to wear our sorrow on our sleeves; we can convey our emotions in safe ways. We can share our emotions with people we feel comfortable with: trusted friends, clergymembers, therapists or support group members.

I am brave enough to feel my emotions and express them appropriately.

UNDERSTAND THOSE WHO GRIEVE WITH YOU
— ⚹ —

Family dynamics play a part in how you and your relatives respond to losses. In a family, members play different roles: Someone takes care of everybody. Someone avoids responsibility. Someone fixes things. Someone always gets the blame. Someone gets all the attention.

Try to understand what your position has been in your family. It will help you better comprehend what you are going through now. Also, try to understand the role everyone else has played. Perhaps knowing that your older sister always has to be the boss will help you be kind to her when she tries to take over family responsibilities during your loss. Now is not the time to try to point out the error of her ways. When people are hurting, they fall back on old coping skills. The controller of the family might become extra controlling. If that's how she got through most of her life, don't expect her to change now. As a matter of fact, expect that she will be even more controlling.

We tend to believe that our way of doing things, including mourning, is the right way. Other people have a right to respond to a death in whatever way feels right for them. Don't make the mistake of thinking that if someone doesn't cry, she isn't sad. Don't assume that if someone wants to rush through the funeral, he didn't love the person who died. But even if time or experience confirms your suspicions, let people be.

After my friend Karen's mother died, she and her siblings had to confront their different styles of grieving. Karen said, "One thing we've learned is that even though we come from the same gene pool, my brother, my sister and I are totally different. We do everything differently. Why shouldn't we grieve differently too? The key is that we all loved our mother and she loved all of us."

If you are worried about how someone is coping, all you can do is be there for them. You can listen to them. You can share inspirational writings. You can pray for them. But you can't tell them how to grieve or take away their pain.

If the person isn't functioning (hasn't left home in ages, is spending weeks in bed), talk to your minister, counselor, teacher or a grief therapist. Find out if professional help is needed. If the person seems to be preparing to die (giving away belongings, saying good-bye, saying he wants to be dead) or has threatened to harm himself, call a suicide hot line or behavioral-health center immediately.

After a loss, our weak points will be magnified, as well as our good points. This is also true for our families and friends. Treat your loved ones as you would like to be treated, not by expecting them to behave and feel as you do, but by respecting their individuality.

I love and accept my friends and
family exactly as they are.

TAKE CARE OF YOURSELF

Grief hurts, not just emotionally but physically. We yearn for our loved ones so much we ache. We might have headaches, chest pains or stomachaches. We are susceptible to colds and flu. We might not be able to sleep, or we might want to sleep all the time. We may have no appetite, or we may eat more than usual.

Pay attention to the aches and pains of your body and take care of yourself. If you're "sick with grief," exercise, relaxation techniques and taking multivitamins will help. It might not be a bad idea to see your doctor.

In these first raw days and months, you may be so overwhelmed that you neglect simple things: eating, resting or even breathing properly. Have you eaten something healthy today? Are you keeping so busy that you don't take time to rest? Or are you doing nothing but sleeping?

After my mother died, it felt good to be in or near water. I took baths every day, sometimes twice a day. I spent as much time as possible by neighborhood ponds, and I was fortunate enough to be able to go to a beach in Mexico for a week. I spent most of that time in the ocean where the water was as warm and salty as my tears.

Be good to yourself. What makes you feel better? Listen to your body. Does it need rest, movement, touch? What does your heart want? Laughter, tears, prayer, time alone?

I nurture and nourish myself to get through grief's dark passages.

Exercises

CHRONICLE YOUR JOURNEY
—⚬—

Start a grief journal to keep track of where you are and where you've been. You can use a simple spiral notebook or a leather-bound journal. Be as practical or as fancy as you like. Use your grief journal to write down your feelings (or lack of them) and thoughts. Try to write something every day even if you only write a word or two.

Think of your journal as a safe place to communicate and examine your most disturbing or embarrassing thoughts and feelings. If you've spent a lot of time taking care of a sick person, you might feel relieved that he has passed, giving you back your life. While this is a very natural, human reaction, it's hard to admit to other people. Write about it in your grief journal.

Write about what you were taught about life, grief and death. Write about other losses you've experienced, how you reacted to them and what they meant to you.

Your grief journal is for reflections, rantings, tirades, whispers, sighs, sobs and smiles. Put down anything you want. Write about how, when and where your loved one died. Tell your grief story as many times and in as many ways as you need.

Try it today. Write down a word, a paragraph or a page.

CREATE A GRIEF SANCTUARY

We need figurative space to work through grief, as well as literal space, which is why I suggest creating a grief sanctuary.

You can designate an entire room as the place where you grieve, or you can create an altar in a quiet room. Use pictures of the departed, one of his favorite possessions, candles or incense, flowers, plants, stones, shells or feathers. I chose the bathroom as my sanctuary for its privacy, and because I felt more comfortable crying while in the tub or shower. I also placed a photo of my mother holding her fingers in the peace sign, candles, and a few keepsakes from her in the living room, where I could see them often, and share them with others.

Make sure your sanctuary has a comfortable chair or a floor mat (or, like me, use the tub) for prayer and meditation. Keep a box of tissues there. Place an inspirational quote on the wall or in a picture frame.

Most important, make sure you feel safe enough to explore your emotions.

WRITE A LETTER TO YOUR LOVED ONE

Writing letters to people is a helpful method of divulging distressing emotions, even to someone who has died. This exercise is a good one to repeat, as you probably will have much to say as you travel through grief. In your letters, share your love, regrets, anger, hurt, longing and other feelings. Pay tribute. Write poetry. Tell stories. Say all the things you have left unsaid.

You can write letters in your journal and keep them. Or you can place them on the altar of your grief sanctuary or place the letters on your loved one's grave. The first time I visited my mother's grave, I left her a letter asking her forgiveness for all the ways I let her down and telling her that I forgave her for all the ways she had hurt me. The ground was wet, and when I laid the letter on the headstone, the purple ink ran, as did my tears. I cried and cried, and felt relieved of some of my guilt and resentment.

If you have business you'd like to finish with the deceased or if you need to say something painful or unsettling, you can burn your letters, tear them up or bury them to symbolically put matters to rest.

JOIN (OR START) A GRIEF SUPPORT GROUP

My family and friends helped me greatly while I grieved, but I sometimes needed more attention than they could give. So I joined a support group through a local hospice organization. It was incredible to be with other people who, because they were also newly bereaved, knew exactly what I meant when I shared my feelings about the loss of my mother. The group facilitators and members understood and respected my grief and also showed me that I would make it through this journey. Every week, I was reminded that it takes time (much more than most people think) and work (much more than most want to do) to restore a broken soul.

Check your newspaper for listings of support groups. Ask your minister or call hospitals to find out if they have support groups.

If you can't find a group that is compatible with your needs, start one. Talk to people you know who have recently lost someone and see if they would be interested in getting together once a week or once a month to talk about how they feel. Put together a flyer to hand out at churches, hospitals and mortuaries.

AFFIRM THE POSITIVE

It can be difficult to see the positive in life when we are grieving. It can be almost impossible to believe that we will stop feeling downhearted. One way to convince ourselves of our ability to heal is to say and write affirmations.

Affirmations are positive statements of things that are true (or that we would like to be true) about our lives. Affirmations work by changing our thinking, which in turn can change our feelings and actions. Saying affirmations won't deliver a million dollars to your front door. Nor will affirmations end your grief before you have worked through it. But thinking and acting positively can help make your grief work more bearable.

There are affirmations at the end of each meditation in this book, and here are some more that may help:

- I am at peace.

- I am right where I'm supposed to be.

- I am whole just as I am.

- I am complete in God's love.

- I radiate universal wisdom and love.

- The spirit of God is inside me.

- God watches over me.

- I accept all my emotions.

- I deserve love, serenity and happiness.

- Every day, I grow wiser, stronger and more loving.

—m—

THE MIDDLE PASSAGE

Adjusting to Life Without Your Loved One

God of our weary years,

God of our silent tears,

Thou who hast brought us thus far on the way

Thou who hast by Thy might

Led us into the light,

Keep us forever in the path, we pray.

"Lift Every Voice and Sing,"
JAMES WELDON JOHNSON

This middle part of the journey through grief is marked by longing, hopelessness and fatigue. We are bone tired. Tired of treading bitter waters. Still bewildered by this peculiar world without our loved ones, we now must live with the daily battering of the reality of our loss.

The middle passage is the longest, and, maybe, hardest part of the journey. It was for the men, women and children packed like sardines into ships that left the freedom of Africa for the bondage of America. And it is for those of us traveling from the safety of our loved one's presence into the emptiness of life without them.

Part of what makes the middle passage so hard is that it lasts so long that we become unsure of ourselves. During this low point, people might confront you about how you are grieving. When you have merciful respites from grief's stranglehold, they might interpret your joy or relaxed demeanor as disrespect for the dead. Please don't let anybody steal your peace of mind. You know how precious and rare it is to feel good; when you do, enjoy it. Conversely, as time passes, you might feel pressure from others to be "over it." There's just no pleasing some people.

All this could make you start to wonder if something is wrong with you because you haven't yet moved beyond your grief. Or it could make you feel guilty when you are occasionally able to walk away from sorrow, afraid that you will betray your loved one by moving forward. Or it could make you afraid that letting go of grief means letting go of the person you lost. But remember, you're entitled to travel this journey at your own pace.

Suffering the loss of a loved one is one of the hardest things you will do. It takes willingness, courage and faith. You are on a journey that will take you across an ocean of pain and through deep valleys and shadowy woods. Ultimately, this journey is one of self-

Meditations

DEPRESSION

"Good morning heartache," sang Billie Holiday. We who travel grief's path also greet each day with a familiar, unbearable sadness that weighs on our hearts.

Grief makes us feel hopeless, sluggish, apathetic. Food, music, sex, hobbies and friends no longer give us pleasure.

How long these feelings last varies from person to person. However, it's common for people to feel depressed for months. And some people may suffer from grief depression off and on for years. But while it may not feel like it, grief depression, unlike clinical depression, is temporary. It *does* end. You may not believe it now, but you will delight in life again. Food will taste good again. Favorite songs will make you want to dance again.

Ms. Holiday's song tells a truth: Embracing sorrow can lead to healing. Welcome pain and know that when you learn its lesson, you will let go of it. Know that in time you will say good-bye to heartache.

My spirit aches now, but I will again sing songs of joy.

The hoopla of the funeral has died down and relatives and friends have returned to the business of their own lives. In addition, now that we are no longer distracted by funeral arrangements and other decisions that must be made immediately after a loss we are all too aware that our loved ones aren't here anymore.

Some say that ultimately we are all alone. We come into this world and leave it on our own. But I believe the spirits of our foremothers and -fathers are always with us.

As my mother was dying, blinded by cancer, she kept asking who was in the room with her. Once she asked, "Who's in here wearing a blue outfit?" I told her I didn't know and asked who she saw. She wouldn't answer me, but told me she could "see" things with her mind's eye.

Hospice nurses, volunteers and others who work with terminally ill people will tell you many such stories. Scientists speculate that these visions are hallucinations born of pain medication, brain malfunctions or psychological cushioning to help deal with the awesomeness of our own mortality.

But I was there. I felt the energy in the room. I heard the truth in my mother's voice. People (Spirits? Angels?) were shepherding my mother from one life to the next, helping her cross over. That's what she saw. And, if those beings are there for us when it's time to die, I have to believe they are there to help during this crossing as well.

If you feel lonely, it might help to have someone stay at your house or to be with you during particularly rough times of the day (such as when everyone else in your household is at work or school or the time of day your loved one passed away) for a while. If nighttime is rough for you, drink a glass of warm milk or decaffeinated tea before you go to bed to help you sleep through the night. Keep a night-light on in the hallway or bathroom. If you like sound, sleep with the TV or radio on.

You might also think about getting a pet. Numerous studies have shown that taking care of animals makes people feel better, and pets are easy company, requiring little in return for the affection and companionship they offer.

I know you feel alone now. And I know it hurts, but you're not alone. Those who have gone before you are watching over you and wishing you well.

I am never alone. My higher power and my loved one's spirit are always with me.

WITHDRAWAL
—w—

Sometimes we'll feel lonely, but at other points in our journey, we may be unable to tolerate company. The support
and care we craved may start to work our nerves and make
us want to be left alone. Being with folks can tax the little
stores of energy we have, making us feel a need to shrink
away from talk, activity and attention. Our detachment is a
natural reaction to our intuitive need to go within to heal
ourselves.

Don't be afraid to be protective of your time and energy. If you want time alone, take it. My friend Catherine
said that while she was mourning the loss of her mother, she
needed a lot of time alone. And when she did spend time
with people, it was only with her closest friends and relatives.

I know I've said it before, but we have a duty to
ourselves to honor what we need to do to get better. In
the long run, we'll be better spouses, friends and parents
if we take care of ourselves. Part of taking care of ourselves
is seeking plenty of solitude and quiet when we need it.

*I give myself as much rest and quiet
as I need.*

How can we pray for our own healing when our prayers that our loved ones would be cured weren't answered? How can we pray to accept the truth of our loss when we prayed that the news of their death wasn't true? How can we hope for the future when our hopes for our loved ones have been shattered?

It's easy to accept that misery is a part of life when tragedy happens to other people; then pain is theoretical. But when disaster strikes those we care about or happens to us, pain becomes too much to accept.

With all the adversity we face, I don't know how black folks continue to pray. I don't know how our people have maintained their faith in goodness when we have such evidence of the harshness and cruelty of life. But somehow we continue to have faith. I don't even understand my own faith, but I'm grateful for it. I'm grateful that I come from a people that no matter how many times life knocks us down, we believe we will rise again. I'm grateful that I've seen my grandmother and grandfather be able to praise God even though they've outlived their parents, some of their sisters and brothers, many of their friends and two of their children. I'm grateful that my faith has been big enough and wide enough to allow for doubts. I'm grateful that when I'm having a "dark night of the soul," there's a part of me that is able to light a candle and hold on until morning.

If your faith has been shaken by loss, don't be ashamed or worried. It's normal, and you are all right. If you can't pray or don't want to pray right now, you don't have to. Instead of talking to God, talk to nature. Tell the moon your sorrows. Ask the stars to watch over you.

Your heart aches now, but your trust in God and life is still in you and it will see you through. You may not believe it now, but you will remember how to hope again. You will hold on until dawn.

My faith is strong enough to withstand my grief.

GRIEF AND SPIRITUALITY

We may feel guilty about mourning if we consider our-selves religious or spiritual. We may wonder how we can believe in God's love or a divine plan for our lives while feeling so terrible now. Faith has brought our people far. We've weathered many storms by believing in a higher purpose and meaning. But having faith doesn't mean losses don't hurt. Faith doesn't mean we won't miss those who have gone home. Even the Bible says, "Blessed are they that mourn: for they shall be comforted" (Matthew 5:4).

Faith means knowing that while you are mourning you are being held in God's love. Faith means that even though we can't understand why we have lost our loved ones and even though we'll never be happy about their loss, we embrace today as a means of getting to tomorrow, knowing that each event in our lives is a bridge to our future.

You already are going through so much. Don't add to your suffering by imagining that you should be above or beyond sorrow. Lean on your faith for comfort, but don't hide behind it. Mourn bravely, knowing it is healthy, necessary and your right.

I believe in God and my right to grieve.

DIVINE TIMING
—⟋⟍—

I don't pretend to know God's plan for us. But I do trust that there is a reason we experience sorrow as well as joy. Maybe sorrow allows us to truly appreciate good times. We are quick to take things for granted, so maybe a little darkness is a good way to help us be grateful for the light. We always seem to learn our lessons best when faced with hardship and challenge. I know I listen and learn faster when my back is up against the wall or my heart is on the floor.

But believing there's a reason for pain doesn't make it go away. It still hurts to have lost my mother, as I'm sure your loss still hurts.

Let it be some comfort that though you are in the time of mourning, the time to be healed, even to dance, *will* come. Universal wisdom says it must. Remember Ecclesiastes 3:1-8: "To every thing there is a season, and a time to every purpose under the heavens . . . A time to weep, and a time to laugh; a time to mourn, and a time to dance. . . ."

In the meantime, handle each moment as it arrives. Seek solace from your family and friends. Cherish your memories and keep them close to your heart.

Hang on. This too shall pass. You *will* get through this. One tear, one hope, one prayer at a time.

My life is on a divine schedule. I know that healing will come in its own time.

SOME MYTHS ABOUT THE GRIEF JOURNEY

Time heals all wounds. If we don't think about our pain, it'll go away. Grief lasts for a year. We go through each stage of grief in a certain order and then we're done.

Yeah, right.

By now, you know better. You know that yes, time helps us heal, but recovery is not a simple process. You know that ignoring your misery will not make it go away. It might seem so for a while, but it comes out in other ways. My best friend was ten years old when her father was murdered. As a child, she was unable to process her grief. Eighteen years later at my mother's funeral she cried harder than I did. That year, she visited her father's grave for the first time. Grief doesn't go away with time alone. Without working through our emotions, grief sits there and waits for us.

Use all the information and advice about grief you find helpful. It was useful for me to know what grief counselors and psychologists say about grief. It helped validate the emotions I was having and the manner in which they came at me. But be careful when comparing yourself to others. Your grief journey is unique to you.

I make up my own mind about my grief journey.

THE ONLY WAY OUT IS THROUGH

The grief journey can be confusing, frustrating and scary. There is no trick for getting around grief, we simply must go through it. Even all the tips in this book cannot help you sidestep it. Nor will the support and prayers from your friends. Nor will divine love. We have to experience grief's many twists and turns, but thankfully, the journey becomes more manageable and less scary.

Many days during the middle of my grief journey, I woke up to find myself depressed again; angry at myself that I was still angry at my mother or God for putting me through hell. For so long I just wanted to be done with it. I tried to escape my grief through exercise, writing, eating and sleeping. These activities do help immensely. The journey is much easier when we are physically and emotionally healthy. But there are no shortcuts.

We can't rush or circumvent grief, but we can encourage healing. Love yourself. Accept all of your emotions. Let people care for you. And know you will experience as much as you need to learn and grow.

No matter where you are in your grief journey, take heart that you are right where you should be. Don't be frustrated by setbacks. For every two steps forward, there may be one step back. But you *are* making progress.

Each day I celebrate that I am farther along in my grief journey.

UNFINISHED BUSINESS

It's rare for us to be granted the time and opportunity to work through all our issues with someone before they die. Almost all of us will have some unfinished business with our loved ones: feelings left unshared, issues left unresolved.

When people die, we mourn more than their loss. We mourn all they have meant to us—good and bad—and all that the relationship never was and might have been. We will have to let go of the hopes and expectations we had of the person. We will have to let go of the plans and dreams we shared with them. In her book, *I Asked for Intimacy*, the Reverend Renita J. Weems writes about her struggle to accept her mother's alcoholism after her mother's death. Like her, you might have to mourn the challenges your loved one never overcame.

Writing letters to say the things you never got to say helps. Seeing a therapist also can help. Even then, you may not ever fully finish things with your loved one, but unfinished business need not stand in the way of resolving your grief. You may not achieve closure with your loved ones, but slowly, surely you can move on.

I may not have said everything I wanted to say to my loved one, but I can still progress in my grief journey.

IDEALIZATION

Because we miss our loved ones, it's easy to dwell on their positive characteristics and forget their faults. It is comforting to focus on happy memories. Forgiving their weaknesses and celebrating their strength, integrity, humor, faithfulness or other good traits is a way to honor those who go before us. But sometimes we go overboard and start to believe our loved ones were pillars of virtue. This is called idealization.

It's natural for us to want to focus on the best about our loved ones, but we don't do ourselves any good pretending they were saints. It limits our healing process; we can't completely mourn their deaths if we aren't being realistic about their lives. We don't need to idealize our loved ones; we can fully mourn them exactly as they were: flawed and human.

Certainly, our Creator doesn't expect to welcome only perfect people into the next life. Why should we think we can only say good-bye to perfect people? Nobody is without fault. We all leave behind people we disappointed, insulted, embarrassed, deceived or hurt in some way.

Be respectful of those who have passed on. Cherish the good times. Show gratitude for all they gave you. But be careful to also be truthful about your relationships. You honor yourself and the deceased with honest regard.

I respect my loved one and myself
enough to remember my loved
one truthfully.

COMMUNION
—⠶⠶—

I still talk to my mother. I ask her questions, tell her what's happening in my life, especially things that would make her laugh, like the fact that the older I get, the wiser she seems.

Sometimes my mother's spirit feels very near. Sometimes I doubt her presence. But it almost doesn't matter whether I can sense her or not. It still makes me feel better to talk to her. So when I feel like talking to my mother, I do . . . driving down the street, baking a cake, hiking in the mountains.

Communing with her in this way will never be as satisfying as curling up next to her on the couch. It will never be as lively as our regular phone conversations. For those who have lost husbands or wives, communing with their spirits will never be as comforting as their spouses' touch. For those who have lost children, it will never be as warm as their sleeping children's soft breath. But, we can hold on to the belief that our departed loved ones are still a part of our lives.

My spirit and the spirit of my loved one are forever connected.

MOURNING RITUALS

There is a difference between grief and mourning. Grief is what we feel after the death of someone we care about. Mourning is how we express those feelings.

Mourning is active: wearing a certain color to the funeral to show respect for the dead or reverence for life; falling out crying; saying a prayer for your loved one. Mourning is the New Orleans funeral procession that sings slow and deep on the way to the cemetery and dances merrily all the way back, lamenting death and celebrating life at the same time. It's the flowers, toys and letters people left at the site of the Oklahoma City bombing. It's the "stop the violence" murals painted on buildings in inner-city neighborhoods. It's candlelight vigils, marches and rallies.

In addition to helping us honor the dead, mourning also enables us to heal. We must express how we feel to adapt to our losses and move forward. People who don't face their emotions and deal with them only slow the process of healing. Unresolved grief can hinder relationships and keep us from happy, successful lives.

Mourning rituals such as wakes, funerals and memorial services give us times and places to acknowledge death. They give us permission to express how we feel. However, we are not done with grief and mourning after these ceremonies. Our loved ones have been given back to the earth, floated across water or wafted through the air, but our mourning may be just beginning.

It helps to develop less formal rituals. Lighting a candle for your loved one is a ritual. Setting a place at the dinner table for your loved one during celebrations is a ritual. Kissing a photo of your loved one every night before you go to sleep is a ritual. All of these acts express the loneliness you feel without your loved one and the gratefulness you felt to have them while they were here.

It also helps to mourn with others. Encourage other relatives and friends who share your loss to talk about their feelings. Bring people together for rituals; the spirit of fellowship can make them more powerful. Incorporate readings, stories about your loved one, prayers, music and moments of silence.

However, be careful not to let rituals keep you from grieving. Don't get so caught up in preparing just the "right" ritual that you neglect the emotional work of grief. Simple is better. Remember, rituals are ways for you to *express* your grief, not suppress it.

I take action to honor my loved one
and heal myself.

FINDING MEANING
—ʍ—

When someone we love dies, we want to understand it. What does it mean? Why did it happen?

One reason we search for answers is because we think by understanding we can protect ourselves from future losses. We think: Next time, we'll do it right, and then we won't have to hurt like this. But of course, there's no way to ensure we never experience hurt again. Loss is a part of life, and bad things do happen to good people. We might also worry that we're bad people. We might suspect our loss is some kind of karmic debt we must pay for the wrongs we have done, which also is untrue.

But this questioning can lead us to positive insights. Even questioning our spiritual beliefs can make our faith stronger, if for no other reason than we are reminded that there are some questions to which we may never know the answers.

My mother and I were both so young when she died, she forty-five and I twenty-eight, that her death was doubly shocking to me. It shattered my illusion that I'd live forever, and led me to reexamine the choices I was making in my life.

After a loved one passes away, we can look to them as examples of how we should live. We can honor the deceased by continuing to live as they taught us.

We can look back on their lives and remember their creativity, wisdom, integrity or elegance, and strive to live up to their examples.

If the person who passed on lived a less than honorable life or his poor choices even cost him his life, we also have a lesson to learn. Instead of passing judgment, we would do well to ask ourselves if we are making wise choices in our own lives. Are we are living honestly, lovingly and purposefully?

As I grieve, I learn more about life and more about myself.

Exploring sadness, depression and other unpleasant feelings takes courage. We have to be brave to go into the dark places and see what's there.

Embracing pain, rather than avoiding it, is an essential element of grieving well. Of course, even when we try to avoid experiencing the pain of loss, it is always with us. We may as well choose to learn from it. But, I must admit that's tough advice to follow. One day soon after my mother crossed over, I spent $115 on perfume and scented body cream, even though I don't often wear perfume. Later, I realized the primary appeal of the cologne was its name: Escape.

If you are uncomfortable with expressing your emotions, crying, laughing or raging can take courage right now. Reading this book, writing in your grief journal and talking about loss and grief are brave things to do. But even simply getting through one more day can feel like a major effort. And it is major! Surviving your grief is not easy. Never discount how much work it takes you to get through the hurt. Be proud of yourself for hanging in there.

Don't be afraid of your emotions. Honor the process of grief even when you don't understand it. Trust that something positive will come from this sad quest.

I am brave enough to mourn.

MOVING ON
—︎⚬︎—

While my mother was dying, I had two prayers: "God, please don't let my mother die" and "God, please let her die soon." I couldn't stand the thought of her dying, but I also couldn't stand seeing her in pain and watching her leave me. Maybe you understand the contradiction.

Sometimes, what we hope for we also fear.

In grief, we often want our burden lifted even as we fear moving on without it. What will life be like without the companionship of our grief? Who will we be if we are no longer bereaved? Maybe most of all: Will we remember our late loved ones if we don't have sorrow as a reminder?

Rest assured that you will not forsake your loved one by getting on with your life. When you are ready, you will be able to move forward *and* still keep your loved one's memory close to your heart. Don't be afraid to hope for resolution of your grief. It's what your loved one wants for you and it's what your Creator wants for you.

It's OK for me to move forward,
and when I'm ready, I will.

ANNIVERSARIES
—⟋∭⟍—

Every day after my mother died was bad, but Fridays were the worst. On Mondays, Tuesdays and Wednesdays, I was able to do what I needed to do to get through the day. I cleaned house. I cooked meals. I went to the gym. I read or watched movies. Thursdays I didn't feel so good. On Fridays, I could hardly get out of bed; it hurt to move, to breathe. I felt like my insides were turning into molasses and leaking out of my pores. All I could do was cry or sleep. My mother died on a Friday.

For me, Fridays were anniversaries, and subconsciously I was keeping track of them, reliving every excruciating moment of my mother's death. The first few weeks I didn't know what was going on. I didn't understand why Friday should be so much harder than the other days. But when I discovered the pattern, Fridays became more manageable because I knew what to expect.

I began commemorating her death on Fridays by lighting candles at a beautiful basilica. My mother was Catholic and it helped me feel close to her to be in the church of her faith. I prayed, cried and talked quietly to her. Soon, I began marking her death in months. And though it was still upsetting, I did feel a little better, and Fridays became no worse than any other day.

The day of your loved one's death is just one anniversary you will face. You also may intensely reexperience the day you found out your loved one passed away, the day of the funeral and other events surrounding the death. The one-year anniversaries of all your special days are especially momentous. Our imaginations lead us to expect the worst about anniversaries and make us dread having to relive such harrowing memories. You probably will have a lot of anxiety the first time you face these days. Or you may have high expectations that after a certain amount of time you will finally be "over it" and feel particularly depressed to find you're still grieving.

In my experience, the anticipation of the anniversary or holiday is much more distressing than the actual event. Maybe this is true because whatever painful day I was dreading was never quite as awful as I imagined it would be or maybe because I expended so much energy worrying that by the time the day arrived, I was already emotionally spent.

It helps to plan how you want to commemorate the anniversary of your loved one's death. That will give you some control over what will happen on that day and remove some of your anxiety about what to expect.

On the first anniversary of my mother's death, I wanted to do something illustrative of her spirit: I wore a black lace miniskirt, drank tequila and danced until two A.M.

With forethought, I am able to honor my loved one's memory and myself.

THE HOLIDAY BLUES

It's tough to be alone when songs, movies and commercials say we're supposed to be with family and friends. It can make us even sadder when everybody tells us to be merry and happy. How do we mourn while the rest of the world celebrates?

It helps to keep the holidays simple: Make smaller meals. Invite fewer guests. Ask others to host celebrations or prepare the food. Shop for gifts by catalog, and—sticking to the "simple is better" philosophy—choose small, inexpensive tokens of affection. Ask someone to do your shopping for you. Or choose not to give gifts at all.

You also could decide to celebrate the event in a completely different way. Even little things like changing the place or time you eat and open gifts can make celebrations less painful. For example, try going to a restaurant instead of staying home or gathering for brunch instead of dinner.

Or you may prefer to celebrate as usual. Continuing to do things as you've always done them can be reassuring to relatives and friends (especially children). But don't pretend that something hasn't changed. You'll be setting everyone up for heartache; no matter how much you stay with tradition, it will be all too apparent that your celebration is different without your loved one. Maintain your family's customs, but don't deny that now that your loved one is gone, you feel sad or empty.

Another completely valid option is to skip celebrations altogether. I chose not to celebrate Mother's Day for four years; it was only then that I could acknowledge my stepmother, grandmothers and the other mothers in my life.

I give myself permission to mark special days in the way that feels right to me.

DREAMS

Almost all mourners dream about those who have passed on. Dreams of loved ones being at peace are comforting. About three months after my mother died, I had this amazing dream in which she and I met and talked. She was thrilled to be released from cancer's grip. She was excited to be moving on, and she told me we would see each other again. When I woke, I had the feeling that we had taken a journey together, but I had returned to this world and she had gone on. It was unsettling and soothing at the same time.

But sometimes my dreams made me sad. The recurring dreams in which I would relive her death terrorized me and made for restless, fitful sleep. I was devastated when I dreamed she was still alive only to wake up and realize the truth. I still dream that my mother is alive, but the disappointment when I wake isn't as intense.

Don't be disheartened by dreams—sad or happy. Even the worst dreams are ways for us to work through grief. We are so overwhelmed by longing, confusion and sorrow that we express our emotions even while we sleep. Our dreams are also a way of helping us understand what we aren't able to with our conscious minds.

Dreams are powerful teachers. Keep your grief journal by your bed and write down your dreams as soon as you awake. From time to time, look back over what you've written and look for meaningful symbols and patterns. See what your dreams reveal to you.

I pay attention to the lessons in
my dreams.

TAKE IT ONE DAY AT A TIME

We can get trapped into thinking we always will feel this bad. Grief is easier to manage if you take it bit by bit. One way to do that is to live in the present. Don't try to take on tomorrow. If you feel like hell now, you only have to deal with this day. If you can't even face a whole day, take it minute by minute. Try not to get stuck in the past or jump ahead to the future. Just focus on this day, this hour or this minute. Pay attention to what you are thinking, feeling and doing.

Just focus on where you are now. Breathe through it. Pray through it.

If this moment is peaceful, savor it, but don't be disappointed when it passes. Unfortunately, just like the hard times our happier times will end too. However, rest assured that eventually the happy periods will outweigh the bad.

I travel my grief journey one step at a time.

MAKING CHANGES
—∞—

When loved ones die, it seems there are reminders of them everywhere we turn. Our favorite restaurant. The first present we gave them. A song on the radio. Sights, sounds, smells, even times of day, all make us think of our loved ones.

Sometimes reminders of our loved ones comfort us and help us focus on cheerful memories. Other times, seeing a smiling photograph of our loved one or a favorite item going unused slices our hearts.

In those cases it's easy to think that drastically changing our lives to get rid of reminders of our loss will spare us pain. But it's more helpful in the long run to make only temporary changes. For example, it may help to rearrange things, but don't get rid of them until you are sure you don't want them. If it's too painful to see your loved one's things, pack them and store them. Later, you might discover that they are a source of comfort, rather than pain.

If you had put plans on hold because of a loved one's sickness and want to pursue them now, do so, but be wary about chucking everything without much thought. By all means continue your life. However, only make significant decisions when you are on solid ground. While the heart doesn't follow timetables, grief experts say it is a good idea to wait at least a year before you move, end a relationship, get married, quit a job or make other life-changing decisions.

This would be a good time to reflect on the Serenity Prayer:

> God, grant me the serenity to accept the things
> I cannot change, the courage to change the things
> I can and the wisdom to know the difference.

I make changes thoughtfully and prudently.

GRIEVE WITH PURPOSE

When I knew my mother was going to die, I demanded that if I had to hurt this bad, God had better teach me something. That's what got me through: faith that I would be better for having been open to the pain. I willingly embraced my grief, and, although I thought it would break me at times, I welcomed it as a teacher, and it taught me well.

Mourning became a rich time of being fully aware of my mortality. But it takes more than the knowledge that "tomorrow ain't promised" to fully learn the lessons of grief. It takes a conscious choice to allow death—of a loved one or a dream—to lead us to a rebirth of something higher and better. It takes a conscious choice to grieve with purpose.

We grieve purposefully when we face our pain and learn from it. What can we learn from loss? Death reminds us what is important. It reminds us that we only have a short time here and we'd better make good use of it.

What are your dreams? What are your goals? Who matters to you? Losing someone can bring pettiness and small-mindedness to light. Loss can make us aware of how we should treat others better, ways we should treat ourselves better.

Soon after a loss you may think it's impossible for you to learn anything from it, let alone be wiser or stronger. That's OK. Right now, you don't have to see the possibilities. But try to suspend disbelief and acknowledge that maybe, just maybe, there could be a lesson here.

Grieve with the goal that you want to get something from the pain. Ask for it. Demand it, even.

I am open to the lessons of grief.

KNOW YOUR LIMITS

—ᴍ—

Some days, you still may be too sad, angry, tired or distracted to do much more than get by.

You may be discouraged because you're not able to keep up your usual schedule, but right now it's best for you to honor your need to slow down. Don't be frustrated, worried or embarrassed about not keeping up. There's no shame in honoring your limits. It's up to you to take care of yourself by knowing what you can handle and what you can't.

Your primary "work" now is to learn what your grief journey has to teach you. Remind yourself how busy you really are and let go of any expectations that are too difficult to meet. If you're feeling overwhelmed, don't rush back to the PTA, church choir, neighborhood association or book club. You don't have to completely change your life, but if it all seems like too much, you can make temporary changes to help you adjust.

Knowing and honoring your limits is important and healthy anytime, but crucial now. As African Americans, we often feel pressure to withstand difficulty with pride and strength. Our strength is a blessing, but we also need to ease up on ourselves. Stress is a contributing factor to many illnesses, and we do ourselves no favors by putting more strain on ourselves.

I honor my limits and take care of myself.

In times of stress, we tend to fall back on the coping skills we learned as children. Depending on how we were raised, we may have learned to be aggressive or meek, controlling or cooperative, funny or serious or talkative or quiet. Much of our personalities is a result of how we developed within our families.

If our coping skills are positive and healthy, they can be helpful to us during our grief journey. For example, while growing up I learned to always look for the silver lining, which helped me believe something valuable could come from grief. We may have learned behaviors that protected us as children, but are dysfunctional now. For example, one of my negative coping skills is control. After my mother died, I was frightened by how completely out of control I felt. I reverted back to the domineering behavior of my childhood, but it only stood in the way of my healing. In order to move on, I had to let go and let God take over.

Pay attention to how you act when you're stressed out. Think about the coping skills you developed while growing up. Are they helping you now? If you discover that some of your behaviors actually keep you from resolving grief, let them go.

I handle grief in healthy ways.

TAKE CARE OF BUSINESS AND YOUR GRIEF

We can't put life on hold because we don't feel like living. Instead, we often put our grief on hold, but grief catches up to us. Whether it's months or years, eventually we will have to deal with it. And the longer it's put off, the more intense it will be.

So how do you take care of business and attend to your grief journey? Carve out regular time for yourself. Take "grief breaks" throughout the day. Even five minutes to pray, jot a quick note in your journal, cry or talk to a friend can help.

Grieving on the job is especially tough. We want to do well and be considered responsible, but it's difficult to maintain a professional image with puffy, red eyes or smeared mascara. If you have supportive coworkers, ask them for help. Most people will understand that it's hard to keep track of things when your heart is broken. If you're having problems at work, explain to your boss what you are going through. It also may be a good idea to talk with a person from the human-resources department. Your company may have an employee-assistance program that can help, or you may be able to take a leave of absence until you are more capable of handling your duties.

Here are some additional ideas for grief breaks:

- Before you go to work in the morning, spend a few minutes praying or meditating.

- Cry in the shower.

- Listen to inspirational music or lectures in the car.

- During your breaks at work, go for short walks or find a quiet spot to think or cry.

- Write in your grief journal while the kids are taking a nap.

- If you need permission to cry, watch a tear-jerker.

Taking care of myself while I grieve is taking care of business.

LET OTHERS KNOW HOW TO HELP YOU
—∞—

Our loved ones care about us and are eager to reach out to us, but may not know what to do. They also may be reluctant to offer their assistance for fear of overstepping their boundaries or of making us feel even worse. If we don't tell people what we need, how will they know how to help?

Your friends and relatives probably have told you to let them know if there's anything they could do. Have you? When you feel lonely, do you call and ask a friend to join you for a walk? When you need to rest, do you ask a relative to watch the kids? Have you taken your neighbor up on his offer to help with the yard work?

Sometimes, people may try to help, but do all the wrong things. Maybe they hover when you need privacy or change the subject when you want to talk about the death. Let them know how you feel and what you need from them. Be tactful and polite, but honest. The people who care about you will be grateful to know what they can do to ease your pain.

It's OK to ask for what we want and need while grieving. Not only is it OK, it's necessary.

Leaning on my friends and family for support only makes me stronger.

"Normal" takes on a new meaning when we're experiencing the peaks and valleys of grief. We may have a variety of physical symptoms and emotions. We may have wild mood swings—feeling upbeat one minute and sad the next without even knowing why. We may have frighteningly powerful feelings of sorrow, loneliness, fear or anger.

No matter how weird we seem, almost all of us will work through our grief and survive it with our sanity intact. However, in rare instances, grief becomes enough to send someone dangerously close to the edge. Or sometimes a loss triggers other emotional problems. In those cases, professional intervention is critical. A good therapist or maybe even medication can bring a lost soul back from the abyss.

How do you know if you need professional attention?

- If you are having thoughts of killing yourself.

- If you are violent.

- If you are using drugs or alcohol to cope, or if you develop or relapse into other addictive behaviors like gambling, overspending, over-eating or compulsive sex.

- If the circumstances of the death are particu-larly horrific.

- In any instance when you think it would help.

Even if professional counseling isn't required, it can be helpful. No matter how psychologically together we are, no matter how mature, no matter how spiritual, sometimes life is just too hard. Bereavement can be one of those times.

Don't be embarrassed if you need assistance to get through grief. Ask your minister, hospice center, mental-health center or social-work department for in-formation on finding grief counseling.

I wisely ask for help when I need it.

ACCEPT YOUR MISTAKES

Making mistakes is a fact of life that we usually accept calmly and rationally. However, grief can make us afraid of making mistakes.

As you travel through grief, you will have to make adjustments that are fraught with potential for mistakes. You may have to raise your children by yourself. You may have to learn new skills like handling finances or running a household or business. You may have to tackle psychological challenges like becoming more assertive, outgoing or compassionate. While you are adjusting, you may mess up. It's part of learning.

When you err, be gentle with yourself. You're walking into a brave new world and don't yet know the way. Making a few wrong turns is understandable. Pretty soon, you'll have the lay of the land and be able to walk this new path with confidence and skill.

To help boost your confidence, start a list of your positive attributes. Make a note in your journal every time you are kind, attentive, brave, responsible, loyal, honest or caring. Paying attention to your good points will help erase the negative self-perceptions that sometimes accompany grief.

I lovingly give myself permission to make mistakes.

CELEBRATE HOW FAR YOU'VE COME

How are you doing? Maybe today you're managing things a little better. Maybe today you can go all day with only one nap. Maybe today you can cry for hours and not feel embarrassed or ashamed. Maybe today you can think about your loved one without feeling depressed.

If so, say a prayer of gratitude and write it in your grief journal so on the bad days you'll have proof that good days come too.

Or perhaps this is one of the dark days. It's important to acknowledge days when you feel like you're just barely getting through life. The hardest days are as much a part of the growth process as the easy ones. Remember that yesterday was better, and trust that the days ahead will improve.

Give yourself a pat on the back for whatever you're doing today that would have been tough yesterday. Feel proud of your accomplishments. You're doing very important, tough work. And you *are* making progress.

I celebrate my strength, persistence and courage.

ACCEPT OTHERS

It's worth reiterating that grief stretches families. Life will be easier if you accept that those who mourn with you are probably going to get on your nerves sometimes, as you will sometimes annoy them. You're hurting and they're hurting, and people in pain often aren't nice.

Families commonly squabble over a host of things including funeral arrangements, inheritances and grieving styles. It's easier to bicker over these things than it is to admit jealousy, anger, resentment or feelings of abandonment.

If discussions escalate into arguments, take deep breaths or leave the room to give everyone a chance to calm down. Give people space and time to collect themselves. Before you decide to confront someone, ask yourself if it's worth it.

You want your family and friends to respect your grieving process; do the same for them. Patience, compassion and understanding will help you and your loved ones through this time.

I empathize with the pressure that my loved ones feel and try to reduce their stress, rather than contribute to it.

REACH OUT

They say "water seeks its own level," meaning that people of like minds find one another. I have a friend who attracts crazy people. She's not crazy herself, but she delights in the unusual. She likes quirkiness, and somehow odd people know this and feel welcome around her. Strangers tell her their most bizarre, personal business. Once, we were at a college fraternity party, a man wearing an inner tube over his clothes (this was not a costume party; it wasn't even near Halloween) wove through a large ballroom full of hundreds of people straight to her and asked her to dance.

It's the same with mourners. We find one another. We like to be together because we feel safe and comfortable talking about death, fears, sadness and memories. While writing this book I've attracted people who wanted to share their stories of loss: a nephew shot while breaking into a car, a father whose death made a middle-aged man feel like an orphan, a mother slowly wasting away in a nursing home and so many others.

When you share what is in your heart, you help others open up about their feelings. Give it a try. Reach out to a coworker or a neighbor by talking about your grief. See if it opens space for them to discuss their losses. Your lessons will benefit others too.

By the way, my friend—always willing to take a risk—danced one dance with the inner-tube man, who then turned around and left the party. Apparently, he got what he came for. We, too, can take a chance and make sure those around us get what they need.

I extend a hand to my fellow grief travelers.

Our spirits are weakened by loss. And just as our bodies need plenty of rest and good food, our spirits need nourishment too.

Think about what gives you peace. Reading holy texts? Being with other spiritual people? Long walks in the park?

Try to rely on your spiritual practice, but if you find that what used to bring you solace no longer works, don't panic. Though you used to be able to take your troubles to God on your own, perhaps now you need the support and fellowship of a mosque, church or temple. Or you may feel more comfortable in a nonreligious setting like the outdoors, a support group or a therapist's office. Try to keep an open mind and explore new activities. Ask your friends and family what they do to keep their spirits up. If you're not sure what resources are available, check with your church or local hospice organization.

By boosting your spiritual energy, you will be better able to grieve fully and well. You may not feel energized by spiritual practice right away. For a while, you may feel empty no matter what you do. But keep at it. In time, you will be able to reconnect with Spirit again.

I am recharged with Spirit.

GET SOME EXERCISE

Being active affects our bodies and minds. Have you heard of the "runner's high"? When we exercise, our brains release chemicals called endorphins that make us feel more positive, cheerful and optimistic. But we don't have to be marathon runners to realize the mental and emotional benefits of exercise. By taking long walks, working in the garden or playing with kids, we can reap the same rewards.

You probably won't feel up to intensive exercise sessions, but try taking a short walk every day. Turn on the CD player and dance to some uplifting music for a few minutes each day. Try yoga—it's a gentle form of exercise that many people find quite healing and soothing. By stretching and bending the body and quieting the mind, yoga creates mental, spiritual and physical harmony. Swimming is another soothing exercise. If you can't swim, try holding on to the side of a pool and kicking your legs in the water.

Whatever exercise you choose, try to do a little each day. Once you get moving, you'll be glad you did.

I move my body so that my soul will heal.

PAY ATTENTION TO YOUR BREATHING

When I'm depressed, sorrow weighs heavily on my chest. My lungs squeeze up tight and it's hard to get the air through. I have to be conscious about breathing.

For the bereaved, breathing may be especially laborious because every breath reminds us of life. Our breath also connects us to God, which is why breathing calms us when we are anxious. Become aware of your breathing. Take a deep breath right now. Take another one. Try to expand your lungs and your belly with air. Your breath will help you release emotions. Don't be afraid of whatever feelings arise. You may cry. You may feel angry. That's good. Let your breath take you into the healing arms of your higher power.

With each breath, I am healed.

CRY

In the middle of the journey, when we can tire of tears, it bears repeating the obvious: Crying is crucial to our healing. Mary wept. She cried a mother's tears as she let go of her son. So did the other women at Jesus' feet. So did the mothers and fathers who saw their children sold into slavery. So did the parents of Cynthia Wesley, Addie Mae Collins, Carole Robertson and Denise McNair, the four girls killed in their church in Birmingham, Alabama, during the civil rights movement.

Why are we so afraid to cry? Who told us that showing our sadness means we are weak?

Men, especially, believe they have to be stoic and hide their emotions. But men are no less immune to suffering. A man's heart breaks too. African-American women also sometimes think being strong means not crying. And when we do allow ourselves to cry, we cry alone or with our heads in our hands, ashamed for others to see. While my mother was dying, her best friend and I were talking in the kitchen and I started crying and slid to the floor. Instead of trying to help me up, Kim came down to the carpet and cried with me while I sobbed. She taught me to be unashamed of my tears.

We're sad—off and on—for so long we get scared we'll drown in our own tears. But you won't. Your tears will stop in their own time. In the meantime, give yourself permission to cry as much as you need to. With every tear you are closer to resolving your grief. As Psalm 126 says, "Those who sow in tears will reap with songs of joy."

My tears wash away my sorrow, and in the process I am healed.

LAUGH

Comedy has always been a popular means of vanquishing tragedy in the black community. Comedians from Moms Mabley to Richard Pryor to Chris Rock have built their careers making us laugh at things that—on their own—aren't funny.

Humor saved our family while my mother was dying and after she passed away. Even while cloaked in despair, we managed to find things to laugh at. We told obscene and goofy jokes and warm-hearted stories about the woman who meant so much to us all. We giggled when we found price tags still on most of the things she owned and shoe boxes full of receipts saved in case she found something she liked better. We knew Mom wouldn't have been offended. She was quick-witted and loved to laugh. Indeed, she taught us that searching for the humor in a situation is searching for the positive.

Just as shedding tears helps us heal, so does laughing. But in deep grief we may find it hard to laugh. If you need a good laugh, ask yourself: What funny memories come to mind when I think of my loved one? What were his favorite jokes? Which friends make me laugh? What are my favorite comedies?

While it's important not to hide behind smiles when you're crying inside, laughter is good for the soul.

Allow yourself to cry when you need to *and* laugh when you need to.

I smile knowing that my loved one smiles with me.

Life is about opposites. Day and night. Sun and moon. Life and death. Joy and pain. You can't have one without the other. And no matter how long one lasts, the other is always right behind.

Perhaps we can even go so far as to say that the purpose of pain is to teach us about joy, about the value and sacredness of happiness.

Remember in *The Color Purple,* when Celie and Shug talk about God getting angry when people don't notice a brilliant display of wildflowers? Alice Walker's characters remind us that there are reasons to rejoice all around us; bursts of purple flowers are a celebration we are meant to enjoy, as we are meant to enjoy life.

You may be experiencing great pain now, but there will be joy again. Even if you don't want it. Even if it makes you feel guilty to think of laughing or being happy. There will be a time when the hurt isn't as raw. Life guarantees it. There may even be tiny instances of joy within this sorrow. Cherish them, for they are gifts—God's way of reminding us that we aren't meant to suffer endlessly.

I am grateful for the joy I shared with my loved one and the happiness yet to come.

SURRENDER

Black folks are used to battling our way through life. We've had to fight for the right to be free, to vote and to live where we want. We continue to have to fight to get ahead. Sometimes, we don't know when to stop. When we "hit the wall" we keep right on going, even though we're not getting anywhere. Sometimes it's best to knock down the wall or go over it. But sometimes we must stop at the wall.

Sometimes, we must surrender.

I wish I knew a way to spare you the crushing weight of grief, but the truth is that wall is going to come down no matter what you do. It may disintegrate slowly around you or crash down all at once, but it will fall.

Ironically, surrendering to its fall is what saves us. When we surrender to grief, we go with the flow of universal law. We acknowledge that we are not in control, God is. And it is this act of surrender that allows the Great Spirit to work miracles in our lives.

What a relief! We don't have to control other people. We don't have to control ourselves. We don't even have to control our grief. Surrendering doesn't mean permanent defeat. We do rise from the rubble. Until then, lean on your higher power and rest in faith. Trust this process, and know that everything is for your highest good.

I let go and let God.

Exercises

EDUCATE YOURSELF ABOUT GRIEF

Spend an afternoon in the library and read articles by grief experts and fellow mourners. To find companionship on your journey, read autobiographies and books about grief to see what other people do to cope and how they express their grief.

Here are some suggested books:

Gentle Closings: How to Say Goodbye to Someone You Love, Ted Menten

Good Grief Rituals, Elaine Childs-Gowell

A Grief Observed, C. S. Lewis

Healing After Loss: Daily Meditations for Working Through Grief, Martha Whitmore Hickman

I Asked for Intimacy: Stories of Blessings, Betrayals and Birthings, Reverend Renita J. Weems

Just Us: Overcoming and Understanding Homicidal Loss and Grief, Wanda Henry-Jenkins

Lessons in Living, Susan L. Taylor

Life & Loss: A Guide to Help Grieving Children, Linda Goldman

Life Is Goodbye/Life Is Hello: Grieving Well Through All Kinds of Loss, Alla Bozarth-Campbell

Living Through Personal Crisis, Ann Kaiser Stearns

Motherless Daughters, Hope Edelman

The Mourning Handbook, Helen Fitzgerald

Necessary Losses, Judith Viorst

Recovering from the Loss of a Child, Katherine Fair Donnelly

Recovering from the Loss of a Loved One to AIDS, Katherine Fair Donnelly

Soul Quest: A Healing Journey for Women of the African Diaspora, Denese Shervington and Billie Jean Pace

Suicide Survivors, Adina Wrobleski

Understanding Grief: Helping Yourself Heal, Alan Wolfelt

The Value in the Valley, Iyanla Vanzant

When Bad Things Happen to Good People, Harold S. Kushner

When Parents Die: A Guide for Adults, Edward Myers

Widow: Rebuilding Your Life, Genevieve Davis Ginsburg

ENGAGE IN WATER RITES

As I said before, water is soothing. We are made up of mostly water and so is this planet, so to immerse ourselves in water is to immerse ourselves in the life force. Water literally and symbolically cleanses us.

To tap into water's healing powers, take medicinal baths. Bathe with sea salts and extracts of flowers, plants or trees like eucalyptus, clary sage, lavender, jasmine, marigold, chamomile, tea tree or peppermint. Some herbs will relax and calm you while others will make you more alert and energetic. To find the herbs that will work best for you, go to a health-food store and talk to the person in charge of the vitamin and herb section. I prefer natural products, but sometimes a good old-fashioned bubble bath can feel good. Lighting incense or scented candles can also help soothe, relax or uplift you.

Bathe your body with soap, water, self-love and good wishes. As you wash each part of your body, tell it you love it, pray for its peace and healing. Say affirmations ("I am beautiful inside and outside." "My body, mind and spirit are at peace."). When you are ready to end your bath, imagine tension and worry leaving your body and going down the drain.

You can do the same in the shower. Let the warm waters run over your body, knowing they are healing, cleansing and nurturing you.

MAKE A LIST OF THINGS THAT FEEL GOOD

I used to volunteer at a crisis hot line, and in the training we learned that panicked callers mostly needed to be reminded of their options. When we are worried or depressed, we often forget what can help. This exercise is designed to remind you of good ways to take care of yourself.

In your grief journal write down ten things that you enjoy and commit to do one each day. Here are some suggestions to get you started:

- Rock in a rocking chair.

- Buy flowers (or plant some in your garden).

- Ask someone to massage your shoulders.

- Drink a glass of warm milk or herbal tea before you go to bed.

- Watch a funny movie.

- Listen to soothing or uplifting music.

- Call a friend.

- Hug somebody.

- Sit in the sun or by the fireplace.

- Give someone a compliment.

What else would feel good? Start your list today.

HEAD OUTSIDE

Being outdoors is good for the mind, body and soul. Just like any living thing, we need fresh air and sunshine. And the natural world is supreme evidence of a power greater than ourselves (which we need more than ever while we're grieving). Personally, I like to sit by water. Streams and waterfalls sing songs to me and remind me not to worry. The sound of waves lapping up from the ocean or lakes is soothing and nourishing. Sitting in the sun always renews my faith in the all-seeing, all-knowing power of God.

What's your favorite spot? The mountains, forest, desert, meadow or neighborhood park? Take regular outings to hike, swim, bicycle or simply sit and listen to the wind in the trees.

If you need to stay close to home, tend a small garden or grow houseplants. Growing things reminds us of the cycle of life and gets us back in touch with the basics of earth, water and light. If you don't have a green thumb, go to a park or botanical garden and enjoy the fruits of other people's labor.

CONNECT WITH SPIRITUAL WISDOM

I can't stress too much the importance of spiritual healing. If you enjoy fellowship, nurturing and direction from your church, lean on your brothers and sisters there even more. I know many people who felt like they survived their loss by the grace of God and the support of their congregations.

But whether you go to church or temple or not, there are many avenues by which to deepen your spirituality and nurture yourself. You can pray, meditate, chant, drum, dance, do yoga, use creative visualization or talk to the ancestors.

You can connect with spiritual wisdom through silence, prayer, meditation and visualization, and meet your spirit guide or guardian angel.

Open your heart. Ask questions. Before you go to sleep at night ask for answers and insights. Write down what you remember from your meditations or dreams.

PART THREE

WELCOMING SHORES

Living the Lessons of Grief

Sing a song full of the faith that the dark

past has taught us

Sing a song full of the hope that the

present has brought us.

"Lift Every Voice and Sing,"
JAMES WELDON JOHNSON

At the end of our grief journey, our hearts begin to beat again, and we are able to rejoice in their rhythmic song. We understand the poetry that falls from people's lips because we, again, spout the same fruitful words. The knowledge that sorrow could be waiting around the corner no longer keeps us from moving on; instead it makes us cherish each step.

American shores did not welcome our people, but our ancestors were able to turn their tragedy into triumph. They struggled through adversity and worked hard to make notable contributions that truly made this land theirs.

By doing the deep, important work of grief, we reach shores where, honed by pain and fortified by faith, we, too, can build a new home, one that couldn't have existed without this horrendous ordeal. A home where we are stronger for having been weakened, more confident for having been afraid, and more faithful for having been forced to rely even more on a power greater than ourselves.

Coming home to ourselves after our grief journey is also like coming home after a long, hard day at work. Home is where we feel comfortable, protected and at peace. In *Even the Stars Look Lonesome*, Maya Angelou ruminates about the joys of home: "I find that I am quicker to laugh and much quicker to forgive. I am much happier at receiving small gifts and more delighted to be a donor of large gifts. And all of that because I am settled in my home."

At the beginning of my grief journey, I worried about who I would be without my mother. I lost my identity as a daughter and as a "normal" person and could define myself only as a person in mourning. No matter what question was asked of me—"Do you like this song?" "What did you do last weekend?"—my only answer was "My mother just died."

Being a motherless child consumed me because when she died, I died too. At least a part of me did, the part of me that was my mother's "good girl." It's devastating to lose the part of ourselves that lived only through our loved ones. It's a death that we mourn almost as deeply as the death of our loved ones.

However, you could say we are reborn. On these new shores, grief has become part of us, making us more loving, thoughtful and compassionate. Or as Jean-Paul Sartre put it, "Life begins on the other side of despair."

A few months after my mother died, I started writing, which is something I always wanted to do. I'll never know if I would have found another way to realize my dream. Perhaps I would have found the courage to actually sit down and write (instead of just talking about it) if I hadn't lost my mother, but I'm sure I wouldn't be the woman I became at the end of my journey. Like a muscle first weakened, then strengthened, by exercise, it was in the mending that I was able to grow.

The loss of my mother taught me about the blessings that lie within our challenges. It taught me about humility, patience, gratitude, courage and faith. Maybe most significantly, grief taught me the importance of being awake and present in my life. But I would readily give up the gifts I gained in the last several years if it meant having my mother back. Life, of course, doesn't work that way. Our Creator may want us to learn in joy, but misfortune seems to be what gets our attention.

Maybe you are worried about how you're changing. Let me tell you that in return for all your hard work and sorrow, you will be granted opportunities to explore your gifts. You probably have received many blessings after your loss: cards, flowers, food, money, honors and tributes to your loved ones and the love and support of your relatives and friends. There will be other gifts, such as a new awareness of what you have to offer the world and a deeper appreciation of love. Embracing the deep pain of loss increases our capacity to love. Stretching ourselves into grief's depths makes us limber enough to reach love's heights.

Life has other losses in store for us; losses that will break us again. But we made our way to shore once, and we will again. And it's with that knowledge that we can move forward. Don't feel guilty about moving on. Moving on with life makes us human and whole. Being able to live and love again is a testament to the love between you and the person you lost. And, it's how we can reach out to others to help them heal their pain and stop the cycle of unresolved grief.

This section discusses the transition between the end of the grief journey and the beginning of life's new journey, and the lessons we can learn from painful experiences. Take your time. If you're not yet ready to think about the future, put this book down for a while. Come back to it when you are ready. One day the dark past of your grief journey will enable you to sing a song full of hope for the present. As the Maasai tribe in Kenya says, "Everything has an end," including grief.

Meditations

RELEASING THE PAIN
—✺—

Because we are naturally reluctant to embrace suffering, this book stresses the importance of fully mourning a loss. But don't get me wrong, it is also possible to hold on to grief for too long. There is a time to let go of the pain and begin to rebuild.

Think of it as turning your grief over to God. Be confident that a Higher Power will see you through. If you can't let it go all at once, try to let go in small doses. Just for today, turn your sorrow over to God. If you want, you can pick it back up again tomorrow.

If you're not ready to let go even for a minute, don't feel guilty. Don't feel that something is wrong with you. You will be ready when you are ready and not a minute sooner.

Don't worry about your loved one. When the time comes for you to take flight into your new life, your loved one's spirit will be there to lift you up and watch you soar.

I'll know when it's time to let go of my pain and restart my life.

GRATITUDE

What is there to be grateful for after a loss? Of course, we'll never be grateful that we don't have our loved ones. But, perhaps we were fortunate enough to be able to spend time with them during their last days, giving us a chance to say good-bye. Maybe we can be grateful they died quickly and were spared pain. Maybe we can be grateful they died with dignity. Or maybe we can be grateful for the support we've received after our loss.

One day, we might also be grateful for our grief. After going through a painful experience, people often look back and realize how much stronger it has made them. I'm grateful to be given the insights and opportunities that I've had since the loss of my mother.

Right now, it might be tough to muster an attitude of gratitude. But one day, you'll look back on these sad days and be grateful for all that life gives you—the bitter and the sweet. You'll be grateful for the fire that burns the land, as well as the new life that grows in the rich soil it leaves in its wake.

I am grateful for the journey, as well as for making it home.

LOVE

When we lose someone we love, we feel cheated. Sometimes it seems it would have been so much easier not to have loved at all. At least then we wouldn't have to suffer so much. If this is the price of love, who needs it?

We do.

It's a risk we take every time we connect with someone: They could leave us. They could move, fall out of love, change their minds or . . . die. It's terrifying. But love is always worth the risk. The happiness, tenderness and peace that we knew with our loved ones was worth the pain we feel at their loss. And as Tolstoy said, "Only people who are capable of loving strongly can also suffer great sorrow, but this same necessity of loving serves to counteract their grief and heals them." You have the gift of being able to love deeply though it also means sometimes you will hurt deeply. But think of the alternative.

Hold on to the devotion you feel for your loved one. That love will help see you through your grief. Soon you will be able to answer the enduring question—Is it better to have loved and lost than never to have loved at all?—with a resounding yes.

I am willing to love deeply. I know
it is worth the risk.

BEATUY

Poets, painters, novelists and musicians turn despair into great works of art, discovering in the process that the search for beauty concealed in pain can be healing.

We can help ourselves move through grief by trying to find the beauty in our grief. Focus on the grace of the tender memories of your loved one or the exquisite knowledge that you were blessed with the time you shared with her. Try writing poetry or songs, or sculpting, painting or drawing what your grief looks like.

Perhaps you, too, can turn your grief into the continuing work of art that is your life.

I am willing to see the beauty hidden in the pain.

TRANSFORMATION

Grieving a loss changes us in simple and profound ways. A couch potato may turn off the television for good. A driven, career-oriented person may discover the joys of kicking back.

Almost certainly, small aspects of your life will change. For example, I changed my hair and got new glasses. The way I looked no longer seemed to match the way I felt. You may take up exercise, change the way you dress or redecorate your home.

Grief will affect you on a deeper level too. You may question your faith. You may decide to switch to a different religion or leave religion behind altogether. You may want different things from life than you did before your loved one died. Striving for a bigger car or a house in a better neighborhood might not seem so important.

Loss can leave some people pessimistic and resentful, but we can choose how we will react to our losses. We can choose to see grief as an opportunity to grow.

As the caterpillar transforms into the butterfly in the darkness of its cocoon, the darkness of grief has made me the person I was meant to be.

RESPECT YOUR TRANSFORMATION

After a loss, we first change for the worse. We become anxious, tired, withdrawn, helpless and sad. Our confidence disappears like the sun behind a cloud. Grief casts a dark shadow that makes it difficult to see ourselves. But eventually we begin to improve. Thankful to survive grief, we are more humble, forgiving and sensitive. Thankful to be alive, we are braver, more outgoing, spontaneous and passionate.

I am not the same since my mother's death, but I believe I have changed for the better. Oddly, her death has given me more faith in life. No matter how bad things get, there is a part of me that knows I have the strength to make it. For that knowledge, I am eternally grateful. You, too, have probably discovered strength, wisdom and talent you didn't even know you had.

Whoever the "new you" is, love that person with all your might. You are free to be or do whatever you like. Never let anyone try to put you back in a role you've outgrown. The transformation we experience after a loss is one of life's gifts that we must cherish. You deserve to reap the rewards that come from working through your pain.

I love the person I am, and the
person I am becoming.

RELATIONSHIPS
—\~—

You are learning more about yourself. Who you are. What you want. Where you want to be. You are changing. Why shouldn't your relationships change too?

They may change for the better. Your friends and family may be ecstatic that you are more open-minded, patient, kind or spontaneous. However, your relationships also could change for the worse. People may feel threatened by your new personality. They may worry that you won't love them anymore. They may feel that your new interests are taking you away from them.

Just as your personal transformation has been hard for you, it may be difficult for the people in your life to adjust to your change. After all, they are used to the old you. You'll need to give them time to get to know the new you. Be patient with them.

Unfortunately, you may do all the right things and still not be able to maintain some relationships. There are going to be people who liked you better before you changed. It's part of the process: As we outgrow ideas and patterns of behavior, we also outgrow people. It doesn't mean they are bad or wrong. It certainly doesn't mean we are better than they are. It just means we'll need to spend the next phase of our lives with different people.

I patiently and lovingly allow my friends and family to adjust to my new personality.

REACHING OUT

While grieving, we recede into ourselves. We retreat into darkness. But as we progress in our journey, we seek the light.

Focusing on our relationships is one way to reach out to life. While grieving, we may have neglected those dear to us: Marriages and friendships may have suffered. As we heal, we can repair the schisms and make amends.

In addition, we may be ready to start new relationships. Meeting people and making friends reassures us that we are still lovable, that we still have something to offer. Find others who share your hobbies and interests. Join a book club, choir, bowling league. Take a class in art, history, music, dance, literature, or on computers.

We also can re-evaluate our relationship with our community. As I mentioned earlier, Dee Sumpter started MOM-O after her daughter was killed. One of the organization's purposes is to help others who have suffered losses, but the group also has a more ambitious and inspiring goal: to prevent violence. Amazingly, the members of MOM-O reach out to people similar to those who killed their loved ones.

"We take our pain and suffering and give back love to the community," Ms. Sumpter said. "Who better to teach people to respect life, than those of us who have lost someone to murder?"

Everything you do affects someone else. Keep that in mind as you interact with your families and communities. Volunteer at a hospice, homeless shelter, battered women's shelter or for the American Heart Association, American Cancer Society, sororities, fraternities, or the NAACP. One person shining a light on a situation can make a difference in the lives of many.

When I help others, I also help myself.

WAKE-UP CALLS

It's sad to say, but sometimes it takes something drastic to make us pay attention to our choices in life. Studies show that often fathers (who usually spend less time than mothers with their kids) don't realize how important their children are until their kids grow up. Sometimes, people don't understand how infidelity hurts their lovers until someone cheats on them. And, as you know, losing someone teaches us a great deal.

Our senses become heightened when we are surrounded by sorrow and death. We are so amazingly aware of life. Every choice we make suddenly has so much meaning and value.

On her deathbed, my mother told me she wished she could tell people to live as if they were going to die. I took her advice to heart. I don't want to wait until I have cancer or hypertension or diabetes hanging over me to appreciate how remarkable life is. I pray that my mother knows what a blessing she shared with me. It's my gift to her to honor her insight.

You have the same choice. You can give your loved one the same gift. Let their passing be a wake-up call. Honor their memory by listening to the wisdom they shared or by avoiding their mistakes. You and I are so blessed. We can still choose to eat healthier foods. We can still choose to get off the couch and go for a walk. We can choose to say I forgive you to those who have hurt us. We can choose to make amends to those we have hurt.

We can choose to live as if we are going to die.

Because we are. Whether we are lucky enough to live to see 100 years or whether we get hit by a bus tomorrow, we all will leave this world. Let's make certain we make our time count while we are here.

In honor of my loved one and myself, I live mindfully and joyously.

DREAM NEW DREAMS
—〰—

One of the hardest parts about losing someone is that we lose all the hopes and dreams we had for them and for our lives with them. When a child passes on, we lose the dreams of seeing them graduate, marry and have children of their own. When a husband or wife dies, so does the dream of growing old together.

What did you dream of doing with your loved one? Buying a new house? Moving to a new city? Traveling to exotic lands? Planning their wedding? Giving them grandchildren? It can be hard to let go of even simple dreams like sharing breakfast every day or calling long distance on the weekends.

At the end of our grief journey, we can dream new dreams for ourselves. Our futures may not be what we wished, but they can still be rich and full.

What dreams can you still achieve today? What new dreams do you have?

It is healthy and important for me to dream again.

FORGIVE

Part of what allows us to heal is our ability to come to terms with our anger toward those who died. We learn to accept that they didn't die to spite us. This "slight" becomes easy to forgive, as we know on some level that it's ridiculous to blame our loved ones for dying. However, we also may be angry at them for real grievances; even people who love us dearly and have our best interests at heart sometimes hurt us.

We will need to pardon our loved ones in order to move on, but forgiveness, whether of ourselves or others, doesn't come effortlessly. Forgiving the dead, who aren't here to apologize or right their wrongs, is especially hard. We may have trouble admitting they harmed us; we'd rather remember the Perfect Husband or the Supermom. Or perhaps the wound they left us with is so deep that forgiving them feels like letting them off the hook. Why should we forgive people who did bad things to us? Shouldn't we make them pay? We may hope that holding on to grudges will injure the person who hurt us, but in reality we will only hurt ourselves. When we forgive others, we may free them, but we also free ourselves. We release ourselves from hatred and allow ourselves to mourn, heal and grow.

Granting forgiveness doesn't mean what our loved ones did to us was right. It doesn't mean we have to like or respect them or that we will forget what happened. It certainly doesn't mean that we will never feel upset again. Granting forgiveness means we make a commitment to letting go of our ill feelings and our negative connection to those who hurt us.

How do you begin to forgive? Give yourself time; forgiveness doesn't happen overnight. Talk with someone safe about the wrongs committed against you. Express your emotions to God, a therapist, your minister or support group. Concentrate on yourself and your own healing, not on the other person; leave them to divine justice.

I release my loved one from grudges and release myself from misery.

ACCEPT RESPONSIBILITY
—〰—

We can blame grief for many things—mood swings, irrational fears and behaviors and forgetfulness. While we're grieving, we may not be in control of our emotions and many of our actions, but we are still accountable for what we do and say. Grief or no grief, we must accept the consequences of our actions.

You might have made poor choices that created financial, emotional, vocational or relationship problems. For example, after my mother's death I took a lot of time off from work, leaving me broke for a long time. I wanted to kick myself when I came to the other side of my grief journey and realized what I had done. But then I had to admit to myself that I did the best that I could, and that my only choice was to forgive myself and work on watching my money. You did the best you could, too, and you will need to forgive yourself and accept responsibility for where you are.

The good news is that upon reaching the end of our grief journey, we are stronger. The lessons we learn while grieving give us the power to meet life's challenges. Before our loss, we may have given away our power. Now we know how valuable it is and we know how to use it. Use your power to love, serve, forgive and make amends.

I am responsible for my actions.

THINK ABOUT YOUR LEGACY
—m—

We are here because we stand on the shoulders of those who have gone before us. Our elders worked, fought and loved hard enough to make a place for us in this world. We are their legacy. Whatever we achieve, we owe a debt of gratitude to them.

What is your loved one's legacy? Maybe she raised caring, well-adjusted children or built a successful business or a family home. Or perhaps her legacy is cherished memories or words of wisdom. Even children leave us a history of unconditional love and boundless curiosity from which we can learn.

Now think about your legacy. What do you want to leave behind? Answering that question can help you decide what to work for today. It can help you focus on goals and give your life direction. Honor what your loved one gave you by focusing on what you want to leave behind.

I show my gratitude for the place that was made for me by creating room for those who will follow me.

LET GO OF THE PAST

It's good to remember the debts our ancestors paid for us, but we must use that knowledge to move forward, not as an excuse to stay stuck in the past. In addition, our memories of our loved ones should be fuel for being active and present in our lives, rather than holding us back.

One of the lessons we learn on our grief journey is to let go of the past. Everything that happens to us—good and bad—adds up to make us who we are today. The losses we've experienced, and the lessons we've learned because of them, will always be a part of us. But at some point, we must shift our focus from the past to the present, and again begin to dream of the future.

All that matters, all that we are sure of, is today.

I turn away from the past and turn toward my bright future.

MAKE A COMMITMENT TO YOURSELF
—✺—

At first, we are enthusiastic about our newfound awareness of how incredible life is. How miraculous it is to feel so connected to the creative forces of the universe! We vow to live life with gusto and grace, and to never, ever squander opportunities to love and learn.

But once we have resolved our grief and get back to the business of living again, it's easy to lose that zest for life. We can slip back into taking life for granted, reverting to old thoughts and behaviors. It's the path of least resistance. In order to sustain our new enthusiasm, we will need to renew our pledge to cherish life over and over. We will need to make a lifetime commitment to growth and development.

Preserving our new attitude takes vigilance and dedication. We will need to work hard to stay aware of what we are thinking and feeling, and how we are acting.

You're in this for the long haul; our life's journey doesn't end with the grief journey. Pace yourself. Nourish your sense of wonder. Nurture your self-esteem so that you can continue to believe you are worthy of all the good life has to offer.

I am committed to growth and healing.

LIVE LARGE

—ɷ—

Living large doesn't mean having lots of stuff or having the best house, car or clothes on the block. It's not about being rich and famous. Living large means leaping out of the box in which you've put yourself or allowed others to put you. It means setting yourself free. This world and your role in it is much bigger than you think.

Today, live as big as the Creator meant you to. Think about it: Do you think God created us to suffer, to grovel? No, we were not meant to hide and cower like hunted animals. Lift your head up to the sky and walk in the sunshine.

Have fun. Seek joy. Laugh, play, dance. Enjoy the bountiful harvest God has provided. Set goals and make plans for your future.

You've heard the saying "living well is the best revenge"? Well, living large is the best tribute to your loved one. I know my mother roots for me when I do something bold or brave. Your loved one, too, wants you to embrace life.

I live large and dream big.

Exercises

PICTURE YOUR HOMECOMING
—〰—

Here's a meditation exercise for the end of your journey. Give yourself at least half an hour to do this meditation. Go to your grieving sanctuary. Sit on a chair or pillow on the floor or lie on your bed or on the carpet. (Make yourself comfortable enough so that you will relax, but not so comfortable that you fall asleep.) Light a candle or some incense.

Breathe deeply, and as you begin to relax, focus on your body. Starting from your toes, work your way up through your calves, knees, thighs, behind, hips, stomach, chest, neck, face, and ears to the top of your head. Relaxing each part, breathe in peace, understanding, acceptance and joy, and breathe out sadness, regrets and fear.

When you have relaxed your whole body and are in a peaceful state, summon a picture of what "home" means to you. Home can be where you live now or where you were raised, but it doesn't have to be. Let your imagination describe home to you. Are you outdoors? In a meadow? Near the ocean? On a mountaintop? Are you inside near a cozy fireplace snuggled under a blanket? Are you in Mama's garden or at Grandmama's kitchen table? Are you alone or surrounded by people you love? Take some time to really see, smell and feel your surroundings. Allow yourself to feel the unconditional love radiating around you. Breathe it into your heart and surround yourself in it, until you are glowing like the sunshine, candlelight or warm fire you see.

Now picture your late loved one meeting you there. Know that he is happy and well. Embrace him and tell him that you love him and will always love him. Thank him for all that he has given you, and continues to give you. Tell him that you are leaving grief behind, but you would like him to accompany you on the rest of your life's path. Allow him to welcome you home and listen to what he has to tell you.

As you leave, you're not sad because you know you can return to this place whenever you like because your loved one is always a part of you. Home is always a part of you.

Continue breathing peace and love. After your meditation is over, sit quietly with your feelings and thoughts. Write about what you experience in your grief journal.

REMAKE YOUR GRIEF SANCTUARY

Read through your grief journal and letters that you've written to your loved one. Make a final entry in your journal about what you have learned from grief, and close this journal. Start a new journal by writing down ideas about how to live the lessons of grief.

Meditate or pray. Remember all the moments when you cried and laughed. Remember how hard you thought it would be to survive at times and give thanks that you made it through. Thank God, your loved one, your guardian angel, spirit guide or the ancestors for watching over you. Tell them you have come to the end of your grief journey, and you are embarking on a whole new trip. Ask for their continued guidance.

When you are ready, disassemble your grieving sanctuary or altar. Keep the space for spiritual practice, but change it from a place to mourn to a place to rejoice in life.

Remove items that make you sad. Add fresh flowers or plants to represent new life. Light a candle to symbolize the spirit of your loved one that lives on through you.

COUNT YOUR BLESSINGS

We've heard it a million times, but during difficult times we forget our blessings. Now as you are coming to the other side of grief, think about all the things for which you are grateful. Make a list of your blessings and say a prayer of thanksgiving.

Include on your list:

- Time you had with your loved one.

- Lessons you've learned from your loss.

- People you still have with you.

- Friends and relatives who stood by you.

- New opportunities to give to others.

- Talents and skills you have.

- Health of body and mind.

- Restored energy and balance.

- Hard-earned wisdom and strength.

- A successful grief journey.

CREATE A MISSION STATEMENT

Corporations and small businesses use mission statements to guide the actions and growth of their companies, and to communicate their values and beliefs to the public. Stephen R. Covey, author of *The 7 Habits of Highly Effective People*, suggests that individuals and families write mission statements.

Write an individual mission statement (or one for your family) that details your values and plans for living. Depending on where you are in your grief journey, your mission statement might be something like:

- My mission is to grieve thoroughly and well.

- I am committed to healing and expressing my emotions.

- I honor my loved one by living by the lessons he taught.

With your mission firmly in mind, you can move on with the rest of your life.